20TH-CENTURY COMPOSERS
Béla Bartók

Béla Bartók

by Kenneth Chalmers

To Leanda

Phaidon Press Limited
Regent's Wharf
All Saints Street
London N1 9PA

First published 1995
© 1995 Phaidon Press Limited

ISBN 0 7148 3164 6

A CIP catalogue record for this book is
available from the British Library

Printed in Singapore

Frontispiece, sketch of Bartók
by B. F. Dolbin, 1928

Contents

Preface

Bartók's music belongs to the standard repertoire of orchestras, string quartets, violinists and pianists. While its folk sources are always acknowledged in programme notes, the musical artefact belongs so solidly to the Western classical scene that it is easy to miss just how Hungarian Bartók is. It is common to hear Hungarians express sometimes mild, sometimes strong antipathy to his music; however bewildering this may be to the outsider, there is an element in Bartók which has a resonance only for Hungarians. In this book I have tried to show Bartók in the context of his country and its capital, where he lived for most of his adult life.

Biographies of Bartók often begin with the alarming sentence, 'Béla Bartók was born in Nagyszentmiklós', the name of the town being the unpronounceable Hungarian word Great St Nicholas. This is only one of many such place names and personal names in this book, and so I offer below a short, simplified guide to Hungarian pronunciation, dealing only with vowels and consonants which are significantly different from their English counterparts. Armed with this knowledge the reader can learn to pronounce even the composer's name with the authentic vowels.

Single or double acute accents lengthen a vowel in pronunciation in all cases except *a* and *e*, where they also change the original sound.

a	resembles *o* in *hot*
á	resembles *u* in *hut*
e	resembles *e* in *pen*
é	resembles *a* in *say*
o	resembles *aw* in *paw,* only shorter
ö	resembles *e* in the French *le*
ü	resembles *u* in the French *tu*

c	resembles *ts* in *hats*
cs	resembles *ch* in *church*
gy	resembles *d* in *during*
ny	resembles *n* in *new*
s	resembles *sh* in *ship*
sz	resembles *s* in *sound*
ty	resembles *t* in *student*
j & *ly*	resemble *y* in *yes*
zs	resembles *s* in *pleasure*

Words are always stressed on the first syllable, and a doubled consonant should be pronounced about twice as long as a single one. A few Bartók titles, and the name of one of his contemporaries make a good exercise and illustrate most points:

Öt magyar népdal	Five Hungarian Folk-songs
A Kékszakállú herceg vára	'Duke Bluebeard's Castle'
A kilenc csodaszarvas	'The Nine Enchanted Stags'
Dezső Kosztolányi	

I should like to thank the following: Professor László Somfai and Adrienne Gombocz of the Budapest Bartók Archive for their help with writing this book; Zsusza and James Pontifex and my Hungarian teacher Judit Monori, all of Hungarian Language Services, London; Malcolm Gillies for his suggestions; Paula Kennedy for her help with translations of Hungarian material other than Bartók's letters and writings; Barrie Gavin for lending me his film on the locations of Bartók's field trips; Norman Lebrecht, Peter Owens and the staff of Phaidon Press for their enthusiasm; and my wife Leanda Shrimpton for her work on the Bartók iconography. Quotations of Bartók's correspondence are from *Béla Bartók Letters*, edited by János Demény (London, Faber and Faber, 1971), and writings from *Béla Bartók Essays*, edited by Benjamin Suchoff (London, Faber and Faber, 1976), and I am grateful to the publishers for permission to use this material. I am also grateful to Malcolm Gillies for permission to quote the recollections of Lidi Dósa, Ernő Balogh, Julia Székely and Béla Balázs (all from *Bartók Remembered*), and to George Szirtes and Quartet Books for the paragraph from *Anna Édes*.

Kenneth Chalmers
London, 1995

I

Buda and the Danube viewed
from Gellért Hill, around the
turn of the century

*Little Béla Bartók, a second-year pupil at the
grammar school aroused the audience's interest
when he made his début as a pianist in a guest
appearance. The young genius presented a piece
of his own composition, 'The Course of the
Danube', which also won much applause.*

From *Ugocsa*, the weekly paper of
Ugocsa county, 8 May 1892

Hungary's Future Beethoven 1881–99

Béla Bartók was born into a generation of Hungarian artists and
thinkers at odds with their own country, impatient with the reality
of the present and the image of the past, a generation that set out to
change the cultural and political nature of Hungary. Bartók, Kodály,
the poet Ady, the philosopher Lukács, the painter Berény, and the
'activist' poet, painter and writer Kassák, were all born between 1877
and 1887. Their backgrounds were not at all similar: Kassák started
work as a locksmith's apprentice, Lukács had a privileged, metropolitan background, and Kodály's father was a provincial station-
master. So the fact that Bartók's parents were both teachers does
not reveal much: the overwhelming influence on the young Bartók
was made by his mother, and it was she who determined that her
son's innate musical ability should be developed to the full.

When Bartók was born, on 25 March 1881, Hungary was an apparently stable country within the Habsburg empire, covering a vast area,
and containing numerous ethnic groups and different languages.
Hungarian, a language quite unrelated to any others spoken in the
kingdom, had only recently been modernized and had replaced Latin
as the country's official tongue. However, it was spoken by only forty
per cent of the population: Hungarian-speakers were merely the
largest of a number of ethnic groups, which included Slovakians,
Romanians, Germans, Serbs and Ruthenes (in the area now absorbed
into the Ukraine). In 1848 the lawyer and writer Lajos Kossuth led
a bloodless revolution against Austrian control, which among other
things achieved the emancipation of the peasants from feudal
servitude. The revolution was overturned in the war of the following
year; many of the reforms which had been fought for were reversed,
and an Austrian clamp-down followed. However, such a large area
of opposition to the status quo could not be repressed for ever, and
in 1867 Hungary achieved an historic compromise (*Ausgleich*) with the
Habsburgs, whereby the old Austrian Empire became a joint Austro-
Hungarian monarchy, and Emperor Franz Josef I was declared King
Franz Josef of a Hungary that retained a separate government.

Lajos Kossuth, hero of
Hungarian nationalism and
leader of the 1848 uprising

'One Thousand Years of Statehood': poster for the 1896 Millenium Exhibition, the crowning moment of Hungary's rapid economic growth in the last part of the nineteenth century

German, the first language of bureaucrat immigrants, began to decline as speakers left both their posts and Hungary, and their places were taken either by ethnic Hungarians or by Hungarian-speakers of German origin, or (especially) by Hungarian-speaking Jews, barred as a group from entering politics. Many of the ethnic Hungarians who joined the swelling ranks of the civil service at this time were former landowners who had been bankrupted at the time of the peasants' emancipation, and it is likely that the dead weight of their influence held the country back from developing a social democracy. Only towards the end of the century did an urban, Hungarian-speaking middle class come into existence, and it contained a strong Jewish presence: in the 1880s Jews accounted for a quarter of Budapest's population, but a half of all those eligible to vote. Anti-Semitism, a stain on the country's twentieth-century history, was not a feature of life at this time, at least not in the cities.

Within a generation, in the years of Bartók's childhood and adolescence, the country saw a rapid increase in literacy and industrialization. A comprehensive programme of railway-building in the last

quarter of the century greatly improved communications and facilitated travel between the capital and the countryside. Budapest itself was created in 1873 by joining the two hilly, quaint cities of Buda and Óbuda with the flat, modern urban development of Pest, facing them across the Danube. With the exodus of agricultural workers into this expanding city, and universal access to education, it was only a matter of a generation before a left wing intelligentsia developed. In contrast, the country's establishment remained firmly in the past, believing that to be conservative was to be patriotic. A gulf opened up in the Hungarian consensus, like the Danube dividing Buda and Pest, and the struggles of the early twentieth century between left and right, conservative and progressive, became inevitable.

The Bartók family had its origins in the north of the country, but during the nineteenth century played its part in the colonization by Hungarians of the predominantly Slav and Romanian south. The composer's grandfather had been the headmaster at the agricultural school in Nagyszentmiklós, in what was then the county of Torontál. When he died, four years before the composer was born, his 22-year-old son Béla Senior took over his post.

Postcard of Nagyszentmiklós showing the Agricultural School where Bartók's father was headmaster

Nagyszentmiklósi m. kir. földmives iskola föépülete (igazgatoi lak.)

Nagyszentmiklós was a reasonably large town, with a population of 10,000, chiefly Hungarians, Germans and Romanians. While Hungarian was the official language, there are bound to have been linguistic tensions in the town, and when Hungary was shrunk to a third of its former size by the Treaty of Trianon, leaving not one of Bartók's childhood homes inside its borders, Nagyszentmiklós was ceded to Romania and given its equivalent Romanian name, Sînnicolau Mare (Great St Nicholas). The bickering that surrounded a proposal to erect a plaque commemorating Bartók in his home town in the 1930s indicates a strong residue of linguistic resentment. Bartók insisted that the text on the plaque appear in both Hungarian and Romanian, but this was maliciously interpreted as an insistence that only Hungarian was to be used. The plan dissolved amid the subsequent squabbles.

An insight into the cultural life of this town is provided by Dezső Kosztolányi's satire of turn-of-the-century life and manners in provincial Hungary, *Pacsirta* ('Skylark'). Nagyszentmiklós was a rather smaller place than Kosztolányi's fictitious Sárszeg, and the scale of public entertainments would have been much more limited: there was no theatre, for instance, but there was an amateur orchestra. Bartók's father organized a Music League in 1887, with the intention of improving the existing standard of orchestral playing (he joined the cello section), and young Béla was taken to hear their second performance, given in a local restaurant, on the day after his fifth birthday. At such concerts, Strauss waltzes, Hungarian popular songs and pot-pourris of Italian opera made up the programme, and the boy was particularly struck by the bright, cheerful overture to Rossini's *Semiramide*, the first item on the programme.

Bartók's mother, Paula Voit, grew up in the north of the country, an area incorporated into Czechoslovakia after World War I, now part of Slovakia. Pozsony (modern Bratislava), a city at that stage thoroughly Austro-German in outlook, was the main centre of the area. Her first language was German; she learned Hungarian later, in order to take her teacher's diploma. Her sister Irma, in contrast, had no need to learn Hungarian, and never did so. Paula Bartók, like her husband, was a keen amateur musician, and she arranged for her son's first piano lessons.

In 1921 Mrs Bartók wrote a long reminiscence about her son's earliest years, to amuse her ten-year-old grandson. She starts her account by mentioning the smallpox vaccination Bartók was given at three months, which produced a rash, first on his face, then on his entire body: this lasted until he was five. His parents took him to a doctor in Pest at the age of three, but it was only by being treated with arsenic two years later that the problem began to go away. As the composer's son wrote much later, presumably repeating the story habitually told by family members, 'the permanent itchiness, the people shocked with the sight of the spots, and the many medical treatments without any result made him a reticent child'. Paula Bartók's memoir makes it clear that his musical ability was quickly apparent, and that she helped to develop it. She had the benefit of the child's undivided attention, since he could or would not go out to play with other children because of his rash.

At eighteen months he made his first request for his mother to play a specific piece on the piano. As she recounts: 'I played a dance piece, which he listened to carefully. On the next day he pointed to the piano and motioned (as he still couldn't speak) for me to play. I played several kinds of dance piece, but he shook his head at each one until I presented that particular piece. Then with his smile he indicated "yes".' At three years he could drum the correct beat to any piano piece his mother was playing, and at four he could pick out on the piano what his mother describes as 'folk-songs'. 'When he was sick and had to lie down, he always wanted me either to sing or to tell him a story, and liked it enormously if I stayed beside him. All in all, he loved his mother very, very much – and still does even now, which is my joy. He was always a good, loving son to me.'

Bartók's father died of Addison's disease at the age of thirty-three in August 1888, leaving his widow with two small children; as well as Béla there was a daughter Erzsébet, known as Elza, who was born in 1885. The family remained in Nagyszentmiklós only one more year, while Mrs Bartók started to take piano pupils. Presumably whatever pension she was entitled to was not enough to live on, and it became necessary for her to go back to full-time work; then began the restless criss-crossing of Hungary that characterizes the composer's childhood. Paula Bartók was looking for two things – a good job and the best

Family portraits, clockwise from top: Bartók's mother; Béla aged five; Béla with his sister Elza in 1892; Bartók's father

possible education, particularly musical, for her son. These conditions
only came together in Pozsony five years later, in 1894.

The first post that came up was in the extreme north-east of the
country, in the town of Nagyszőllős, now Vinogradov in the Ukraine.
As she recalled, it was a small place, with no musical life, and she
continued to teach her son at home. Unhappy with the general level
of education, she sent Béla two years later to live with her widowed
sister-in-law, Emma Voit, nearly 200 kilometres away in Nagyvárad
(now the Romanian town of Oradea, near the border between
modern Hungary and Romania), and to attend grammar school there.
Eventually Mrs Bartók decided against the school, finding that the
teachers favoured the children of wealthy parents, and she removed
her son at the end of the 1891–2 school year. Irma Voit, Paula's unmar-
ried sister, joined the family at this point, taking care of the domestic
side of family life while her sister went out to work. Béla's piano
teacher in Nagyvárad, Ferenc Kersch, reportedly taught him a huge
amount of music, but not in any depth: Kersch probably let the
boy race ahead, devouring all the music he came across. Back in
Nagyszőllős Bartók appeared in public for the first time at a charity
concert on 1 May 1892; he played the first movement of Beethoven's
'Waldstein' Sonata, and then, as the local paper reported, 'the young
genius presented a piece of his own composition, "The Course of the
Danube", which also won much applause. Little Béla Bartók's first
public appearance won him several splendid bouquets.' Seven, to be
exact, recorded his mother, one of them made of sweets.

This success prompted Mrs Bartók to apply for one year's leave of
absence, and she returned with her family to her home ground and
the city of Pozsony. It is indicative of her strength of character that she
could leave her job and travel to another city with only the interests of
her gifted son at heart. The trip was undertaken speculatively, after all,
even if it was to familiar territory. By taking this action she helped
to instil in her son a sense of his own importance and the idea that his
musical needs always came first.

Pozsony was an important centre in northern Hungary; during the
Turkish occupation it had been the capital of the country and the
Hungarian kings had traditionally been crowned there, in the Gothic
cathedral of Saint Martin. Sitting on the Danube between Vienna and
Budapest, dominated by its hilltop castle, it was a bustling university

city with a rich ethnic mix and, typically for Central Europe, a long tradition of music-making. Béla started grammar school, with much better results than in Nagyvárad, and took piano lessons privately with Lajos Burger. However, Paula Bartók failed to find the right kind of job there, and after a year she and the family were on the move again. They lived for eight months in Beszterce in the far east of the country (the town is now Bistriţa in Romania). Despite its location, the official language at the time Bartók attended the grammar school there was German, and this was the language he was taught in. Finally, in 1894, a job came up on the staff of the Pozsony teacher-training college, and Paula Bartók moved back to the city permanently. There Bartók finished his secondary education, returning to the Catholic grammar school where the teaching was in Hungarian; a church of the Poor Clares was attached to the school, and in his later years Bartók played the organ here. His musical education was obtained outside school, from László Erkel, son of the leading nineteenth-century composer of Hungarian opera, Ferenc Erkel, and later from Anton Hyrtl.

With Erkel he learned the standard piano repertoire of Clementi's *Gradus ad Parnassum*, Bach's Forty-eight Preludes and Fugues, as well as pieces by Chopin and Liszt. With Hyrtl he did some work on harmony, and came to revere Mendelssohn and Schumann. A friend who was taught piano by Bartók for a while remembered that although he claimed Bach, Beethoven and Brahms to be his idols, the first piece he played at the start of a lesson was by Schumann.

Pozsony was by far the most musical place Bartók had lived in: Paula Bartók had achieved her ambition of providing her son with a stable, musical environment in which his talent could develop. His schooling was now uninterrupted, he had good music teachers, and could hear music played in the homes of the middle-class amateurs of the city. He started to buy scores, his first purchase being Beethoven's overture 'Leonore' No. 3. He instinctively felt the need to compose, and this was something he taught himself from the examples of other works. He stopped writing the dance pieces dedicated to friends and family ('Elza' polka, 'Irma' polka, 'Lajos' valczer), and started to compose sonatas, scherzos, fantasias and capriccios for piano, and later piano and violin.

This choice of genre naturally reflected the music he was hearing in Poszony. All the musical experiences of Bartók's mid-teenage years

Pozsony (Bratislava) on the
Danube, the city where
Bartók attended school. The
castle in the background
was formerly the home of
the Hungarian kings.

were embedded in the prevailing Austro-German tradition, from the
Viennese classics of Mozart and Beethoven to the contemporary
Brahms. A considerable influence on Bartók was made by another
pupil who had passed through the school four years above him, Ernő
Dohnányi, his predecessor in the organ loft, and something of a child
prodigy. Dohnányi went on to study piano and composition at the
Budapest Academy of Music, and on graduating shot to fame playing
Beethoven's G major Piano Concerto in London under one of the
great conducting names of the day, Hans (János) Richter. His opus 1,
a piano quintet written while he was still a student, so impressed
Brahms that he helped to arrange for its first performance, in Vienna.

Bartók's longing to emulate this instant success as a musical all-
rounder accounts for much of what happened over the next few years,
not only his move to Budapest to study piano and composition,
but the rather confused direction of the career he embarked on
after graduating.

Bartók's first opus 1 was a D major waltz he wrote when he was
nine (the Blue Danube floats into view with the second theme).
By the age of thirteen, with a child's mania for listing, he reached
opus 20 – a piano sonata in G minor which he obviously thought
marked the start of a new maturity – and consequently he began
a new list. When he began to study with Hyrtl there was a sudden
flood of music, including, at the age of sixteen, his own attempt at
a piano quintet (Dohnányi's was only two years old). This was
followed a year later by a piano sonata and a piano quartet, faithfully
listed in his school exercise book. The contained romanticism of

Ernő Dohnányi, pianist and
composer, Bartók's early
role-model

Brahms remained Bartók's expressive model for these adolescent
works, music from the opposing Wagnerian camp not being something he could easily have encountered in Pozsony. Wagner had been
dead more than ten years, yet his mature works had still not been
played in the city. It is known that Bartók performed Liszt's piano
transcription of the overture to *Tannhäuser* at a school concert, but the
heady experience of *Tristan* had to wait until he moved to Budapest.

School concerts gave Bartók the opportunity to play his compositions: in March 1898 he performed his Piano Sonata at one, and in
September part of the Piano Quartet was heard at another. He must
have seemed an extraordinarily talented young musician, a natural

Class photo, Pozsony, 1899. Bartók is in the second row from the back, extreme right.

successor to Dohnányi, and the next step was for him to go on to study at a music conservatory.

In December 1898, halfway through his final year at school, Bartók went with his mother to Vienna, to sit the entrance examination for the Conservatory there. Vienna, the city of Brahms, was the very heart of the Austro-German classical tradition, and offered not only a solid, if conventional education, but the cachet of a great musical capital. Bartók passed the exam and was offered a place with a scholarship; but Dohnányi had chosen to study in Budapest, and Bartók was apparently keen to emulate his hero. Consequently, in January 1899 mother and son set off for the Hungarian capital, and Bartók sat an audition at the Academy of Music. Dohnányi's piano teacher István Thomán heard him play Beethoven, Bach, and a Paganini-Liszt study in A minor, and the professor of composition Hans Koessler examined the works he brought. Again he was offered a place and a scholarship, and he decided to accept.

Bartók's preference for Budapest over Vienna is not one a career-minded musician would necessarily have made, and it must be an indication of a growing national awareness in the young composer. But a national identity was an elusive thing in Hungary in the 1890s, even if this was the decade when the country celebrated its millennium. The fragile consensus which existed about the nature of this identity was soon to be blown apart.

In February 1899, only a month after being accepted by the
Budapest Academy, Bartók fell seriously ill: he began to spit blood
and it was suspected that he had tuberculosis. This marked the beginning of a long period of intermittent health problems. He stayed in
bed for a fortnight, but even after getting up was kept off school. He
managed to complete his final year and get good examination results,
but immediately his mother took him off to spend the summer
in Carinthia.

Ill health continued to trouble him after he moved to Budapest
in the autumn to begin his four-year course at the Academy, and
there were prolonged absences here as well. This explains his lifelong
concern for his health; many of the recollections of those people
who knew him refer to his physical frailty, and his first son, Béla,
even wrote an article devoted to the various illnesses Bartók suffered.

At the turn of the century Budapest was determinedly changing
itself into a modern metropolis. Inspired by the grandiose rebuilding
of Vienna, the city had embarked on a massive building programme,
chiefly in the commercial centre of Pest. Everything connected with
progress had its natural home on this side of the Danube: the 1848
revolution started here, and it was the site chosen in 1825 for the
Hungarian Academy of Sciences, symbol of the country's search for
a national identity. The Royal Opera House, the National Theatre,
and the first underground railway in continental Europe were all
built in Pest. It was, and still is, a grand metropolitan centre of boulevards and squares, of imposing buildings and grandiose coffee houses.

Much of the new building of the 1890s was in a Ruritanian
'eclectic' style. Budapest's architects tended to be trained in Vienna,
but when they came home they combined the neo-classicism they had
learned with a style of decoration that was thought to be essentially
Hungarian. The City Park area, the site of the Millennium Exhibition
in 1896, is crowded with examples of this style: the two red-brick
neo-classical buildings at Hősök tér, and behind, the extraordinary
mock-medieval Vajdahunyad Castle (inspired by a real castle in
Transylvania) which sits on a island in the middle of an artificial lake.
Many of the city's other notable buildings date from the same decade.
On the Danube, for instance, is one of the most glaring examples
of eclecticism: the parliament building, based on the Palace of

Vajdahunyad Castle in the City Park area of Budapest. Designed for the Millenium Exhibition by Ignác Alpár, the original temporary structure was so popular that it was replaced by the present permanent building in 1907.

Westminster. And on the opposite bank, in the castle district, behind the mock-Romanesque Fishermen's Bastion (which inspired Disneyland), stands the reconstructed Church of Our Lady (known as the Matthias Church), decorated inside like the illustrations in a nineteenth-century book of fairy-tales.

The Academy of Music had been founded as recently as 1875, and was situated in Pest on the boulevard that leads east from the centre out to the City Park. The first president of the Academy was Ferenc Liszt, who had been born in Hungary but had never had a home there, and although he was recognized as Hungary's greatest composer, Liszt's first language was German: he spoke no Hungarian. His spectacular career as pianist, composer, celebrated lover and flouter of convention had taken him all over Europe, but until the 1870s he had contributed nothing to Hungary's musical life. From 1872, however, he began to spend a part of the year in Budapest, and when the Academy opened he made his home an apartment in the same building, which he kept until his death in 1886.

1896 drawing showing the new underground railway in Budapest (the first in continental Europe) designed by Albert Schickedanz and Fülöp Herzog, running under Andrássy út out to the City Park, site of the Millenium Exhibition. The exhibition encapsulated national pride in Hungary's recent huge technological development.

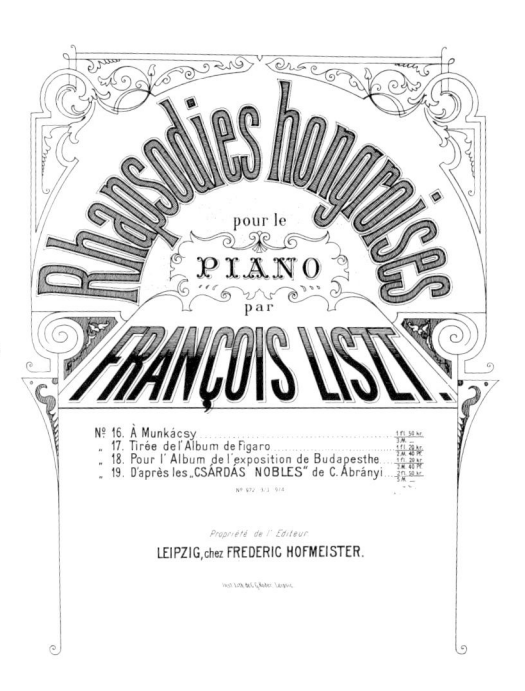

1880 edition of Liszt's immensely popular Hungarian Rhapsodies, which epitomized the gypsy sound accepted at the time as characteristically Hungarian

Bartók's arrival in Budapest was the first time he had been away from the care and attention of his mother, aunts and sister. Within a few weeks he fell ill again with bronchitis, and his mother came up and discussed her son's physical welfare with the Academy. Although she was told he would be advised not to pursue a career in music, she arranged for Béla to be looked after in Buda by her sister, and continue his studies. Afterwards he moved across to Pest, and was cared for by his other aunt, his mother's widowed sister-in-law Emma Voit.

Musical taste among educated people in Budapest was predominantly Germanic, and the only difference from what Bartók had experienced in Pozsony was the accessibility of Wagner's mature music dramas. Audiences at the Opera House were in thrall to Wagner, and

Opposite, 'Liszt and Women': an 1876 caricature showing the musician in clerical dress resisting his band of female admirers

Bartók joined them to hear *Tristan*, *The Mastersingers* and *The Ring*. At that time it was not possible to see *Parsifal* outside Bayreuth, so Bartók did not hear Wagner's last work until he made the customary pilgrimage there in the summer after he graduated, in 1904.

If Budapest music-lovers ever put the Austro-German classical masters aside to play some 'Hungarian' music, they would have reached for the works of Ferenc Erkel or the Hungarian rhapsodies

LISZT és a NŐK.

and dances of Liszt and Brahms. This was an idiom derived from *verbunkos*, a long-established Hungarian dance style, whose roots lay in the Imperial Army's practice of sending recruiting parties round the country – the term derives from the German 'Werbung' (recruiting). While the recruiting soldiers plied their intended victims with drink, gypsy bands would play and the soldiers would perform elaborate dances to impress and ensnare the locals. The music the gypsies played was basically Hungarian folk material embellished with their own virtuosic decorations, and this idiom gradually gelled with nineteenth-century harmony to create an instantly recognizable Hungarian manner, by turns melancholic and frantic, but always quaintly folkloristic. *Verbunkos* itself, a sequence of slow (lassú) and fast (friss) sections, was superseded by the faster *csárdás* dance which became all the rage in Vienna in the 1840s. Erkel's special contribution was to blend this established sound with an Italianate vocal idiom and create a national operatic style.

   In these conditions of certainty about what Hungarian music was, it is easy to see how a gifted musician like Dohnányi had an instant success as a performer and composer following a recognized style. Bartók's gifts were rather different: he was, perhaps, a more analytical pianist, and unquestionably a more searching composer. The way he spent his years at the Academy suggests that he was still following his older colleague's example, but his career did not take off in the same way. It was not only that he was a different kind of musician, but a mood of ferment was starting to shake the foundations in Hungary as the new century dawned, putting all the old certainties into question.

2

A shepherd playing
a *furulya*, a wooden pipe,
photographed by Bartók.

*On one occasion, he heard me singing. I was
singing to the child … The song pleased Bartók,
and he asked me to sing it again because he
wanted to note it down. When he had taken it
down, he went to the piano and played it. He
then called me and asked if he was playing it
properly. Well, it was exactly as I had sung it.*

Lidi Dósa, Bartók's first
folk-song informant

A Red Apple Drops 1899–1907

István Thomán, Bartók's piano professor at the Academy, had
a profound influence on the young man. He started to take a close
interest in his pupil even before he had begun his course, inviting
him to Budapest for a performance of Beethoven's Ninth Symphony,
and generally he watched out for Bartók's welfare during his first years
of study. A letter Bartók wrote to his mother in his first year is full
of references to Thomán's 'good deeds':

> He told me to buy Schubert's Impromptus *as edited by Liszt; when
> I told him no, this month I really couldn't as I had no money, he bought
> them for me 'as a souvenir'. Then he secured free admission to the Sauer
> recital for me, and so I was able to sell the ticket I had already bought.
> And now he's given me a ticket for* The Valkyrie. *He has also mentioned
> the question of the scholarship to the Principal, who said he would very
> much like to award it to me, because he believes that I will fulfil the
> hopes they place in me, but there are a great many candidates ... But
> he said that I should most probably be granted a state bursary.*

Thomán passed on to Bartók the approach to teaching he had
taken from Liszt, whereby the teacher plays a given piece in its
entirety for the pupil to absorb and recreate. The composer's own
pupils describe this as Bartók's method when he went on to teach.
The atmosphere in Thomán's class was warm and supportive, as
Bartók remembered many years later:

> Though Thomán endeavoured to influence with all his knowledge
> and suggestive power the poetical development of the pupil's spiritual
> complexion, he took care that this influence should never be artificial
> but always natural ... As a matter of fact Thomán would play every-
> thing for his pupils at any time and with exemplary patience ...
> Thomán's example as an artist was not to impose ideas on the pupil but
> to awaken the correct ones in him.

This teacher was probably the first adult male to take a close interest in Bartók's development since the death of his father, and Bartók's devotion to Thomán lasted well into his middle age. Thomán also provided musical and social contacts in the city for his student, and this was how Bartók came to have private pupils of his own. He also became involved in the round of musical at-homes hosted by society women who found talented protégés through their contacts with the staff of the Academy. However it is hard to imagine the retiring young provincial as a great social success: music was his only interest. On the social aspects of student life, we can be sure that this 21-year-old is not trying to pull the wool over his doting mother's eyes when he writes home in November 1902, 'I have never had any strong drinks in Budapest so far, although I have often had them offered to me.' 'It's Carnival time, anyway, and spending one's time in the company of young people at this time of year has its dangers, for they will start dancing at the slightest provocation'.

The boy who had confidently composed elaborate chamber music while at school was inevitably more considered and less gushing in what he wrote now that he was a full-time music student. After his first two years at the Academy he stopped writing altogether,

Bartók with his mother and sister in the garden of Aunt Emma's house, 1901

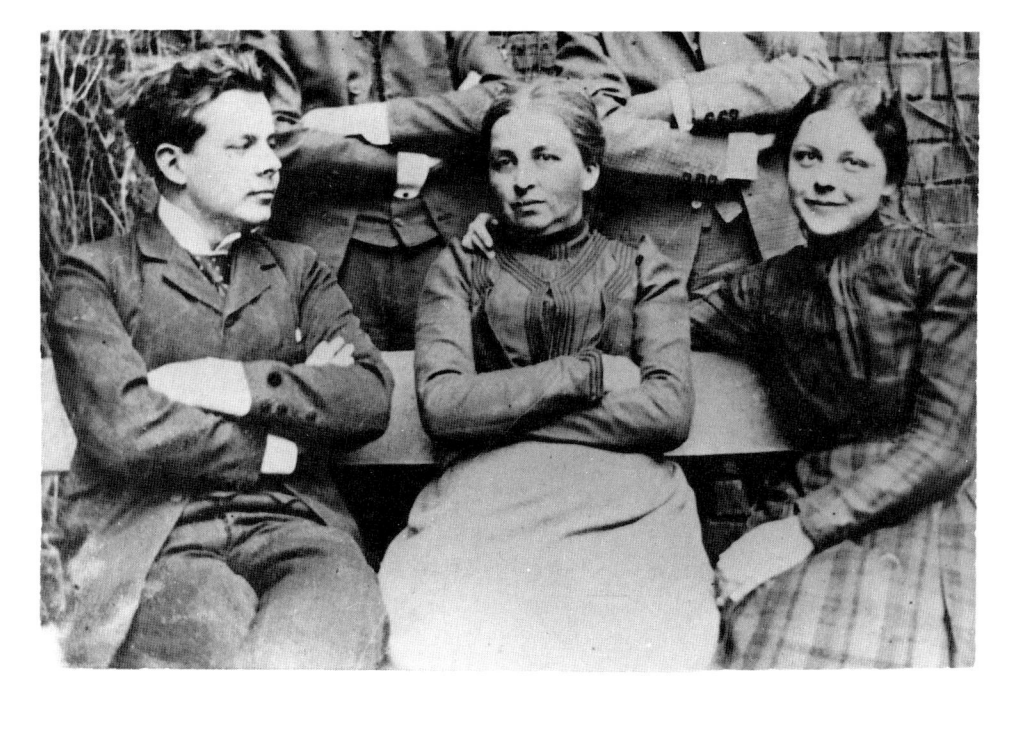

Lunch in Pozsony, with Elza and Aunt Irma, summer 1901. Convalescing after his recent illness, Bartók has a glass of milk on the table.

and Kodály later expressed the opinion that this was because of the limitations of his teacher, Koessler. The problem really lay with Bartók: he needed to be inspired again. It was part of his musical nature every so often to have a strong, creative reaction to some fresh, outside stimulus. Poor Koessler, as conservative in outlook as anyone Bartók would have been exposed to if he had accepted the place offered in Vienna, was typical of his time in representing a certainty and a method that the younger generation increasingly saw as a restriction on freedom of expression. The Academy was the only place in Hungary where music could be studied to degree level, but it was in the business of training teachers and artists, not developing musical thinkers: musicology was not on the curriculum, either at the Academy or the University.

Bartók was certainly making progress as a pianist, and gave his first public performance in Budapest at a students' concert in March 1900, playing the opening movement of Beethoven's C minor Piano Concerto. Thomán accompanied him, playing a reduction of the orchestral part on a second piano.

During the summer holiday following his first year Bartók caught pneumonia and pleurisy, and after a month in bed he was sent to Meran in the south Tyrol (now Merano in Italy) to convalesce. The trip was paid for by Róza Gárdony, his first known patron, one of those hostesses who showered attention on promising music students. He lost nearly two terms of study, and it was not until the spring of the following year that he was strong enough to go back to the Academy. By now his curriculum was complicated by having to repeat classes, but the big event of the autumn term of 1901 was his appearance at an Academy concert, playing Liszt's B minor Sonata, a demanding, virtuoso piece that, by his own admission, he did not fully understand at this time. In November he wrote to his mother that he was planning to study privately with Dohnányi the following summer, and Dohnányi's interpretation of the Liszt Sonata had been a model for his own performance.

Two other important names turn up in the same letter: Bartók mentions that he is to start teaching counterpoint to a certain Mrs Gruber, a friend of Mihalovich, the director of the Academy. Born Emma Sándor, a member of an influential Budapest family, she was at the time the wife of Henrik Gruber, but was later to become Kodály's first wife, and one of the small circle of Bartók's friends. The other name is that of the Arányi family, who had invited him to their house to meet other musicians. There were three daughters in

Bartók is visibly bulkier in this 1901 portrait, taken after returning from four and a half months in the Tyrol, spent recuperating from pleuro-pneumonia.

the family, and Bartók was already teaching piano to the two eldest, one at the Academy and one privately. The youngest daughter, Jelly, later to be one of the great violinists of her time, was only nine years old when Bartók first came to visit. Their father was a police super-intendent, and although Bartók was fascinated by the cheerfulness of the girls and the breadth of their musical circle, he commented that 'they live in rather humble circumstances' and worried about his charges for lessons at home. He was also drawn to the Arányis by their family relation to the great violinist Joachim, and their total ignorance of German. The atmosphere in a home where there were two lively teenage girls must also have been refreshing. In a letter home Bartók chides his mother for describing the Arányis, whom she had not met, as 'cultivated people'. Even from hundreds of miles away she was keen to steer her son towards the right sort of social connections.

The relationship between Bartók and the eldest daughter Adrienne (Adila) developed through at-homes, letters and dedicated violin works into a good friendship, but apparently nothing more. Bartók had already been involved in a sentimental relationship with one of his class mates, Felicitas Fábián, who can be seen in the Thomán class photograph of 1901. The immediately striking thing about the photograph is that women far outnumber men in the class. These women were unlikely to be training to be recitalists, like the Arányi sisters, but they possibly had similar middle-class Jewish families, who would regard a diploma in piano-teaching as an estimable achievement, and an appropriate way of 'finishing' a girl's education.

An entry in the Academy records in Bartók's own writing gives an idea of the repertoire the piano students worked on: plenty of Chopin – Studies, the C sharp minor Nocturne, G flat major *Impromptu* – Schumann *Fantasiestücke*, Schubert-Liszt *Erlkönig*, some Bach Preludes and Fugues (C sharp minor and B flat minor) but not much Beethoven, only the *Diabelli* Variations and the *Rondo a capriccio*, Op. 129.

The rather pale, shy-looking Felicitas Fábián was also a dedicatee of a Bartók composition, in her case, a Scherzo in B flat minor, which starts with the notes F, F, and B, B (B flat in German nomenclature). Just in case she missed the point Bartók wrote their two initials above the stave. There is a German motto, in lines from Goethe:

Richard Strauss, c.1890,
whose music inspired Bartók's
first orchestral works

You give me youth, joy and courage in new songs and dances. Be happy
for ever!

Three years later such a inscription would have been unthinkable,
and he would even be criticizing his mother for speaking to him
in German.

Half-way through his third year at the Academy, in February 1902,
Bartók discovered the music of Richard Strauss. The orchestra of the
Philharmonic Society gave the first Budapest performance of *Also*
sprach Zarathustra that month, and the effect on the twenty-year-old
Bartók of this super-confident work of Nietzsche in musical form
was electric:

István Thomán's piano class
at the Budapest Academy
of Music, 6 June 1901,
with Bartók standing third
from left

The work was received with real abhorrence in musical circles here, but it filled me with the greatest enthusiasm. At last there was a way of composing which seemed to hold the seeds of a new life. At once I threw myself into the study of all Strauss's scores and began again to write music myself.

He wrote this in 1921, in the autobiographical note which he provided for a special issue of the journal *Musikblätter des Anbruch* which his Viennese publisher brought out in honour of his fortieth birthday. The comment comes in the middle of a précis of his musical experiences, so a large element of hindsight is to be expected, but it is true that the discovery of Strauss's music brought a fundamental change in Bartók's musical horizons.

His first creative response to the Strauss was very different from a coyly dedicated Scherzo for a pretty classmate. Bartók embarked on a Symphony in E flat major which he worked on during a summer break spent with the family in Pozsony. He prepared the work in piano score, as he would continue to do with all his subsequent orchestral works, but orchestrated only the Scherzo. This was later performed by the orchestra of the Budapest Opera House in 1904, conducted by István Kerner.

The Strauss score that Bartók most 'threw himself into' was *Ein Heldenleben* ('A Hero's Life') of 1898, an autobiographical work where the composer himself is the hero of the title, and his deeds of heroism include battles with small-minded critics and other opponents. Without hearing a performance of the work, Bartók enthusiastically made a piano transcription – quite a feat to conjure up Strauss's dazzling orchestral sound on a piano – and for this achievement he won the admiration even of his composition teacher, who disapproved of the music. In January of his final year at the Academy he was invited to play the transcription in a concert at one of the temples of Austro-German music, the Tonkünstlerverein in Vienna. This is not to say that the music itself was approved of; on the contrary, it was thought by the musical establishment that Bartók was wasting his great gifts as a pianist in playing Strauss at all.

While Bartók was studying at the Academy, a new nationalist mood had taken hold in Hungary. Political in origin – its roots lay in the simple desire for political autonomy – it soon spread to influence

art and music. The last time there had been any effective defiance
of the Austrians was in 1848, and Bartók's musical response to the
prevailing mood of the early 1900s was to write a symphonic poem
on the hero of that revolution, Lajos Kossuth. *Ein Heldenleben* was
very obviously the model for Bartók, in its division into a number
of descriptive sections, its characterization of an heroic struggle, and
in its massive orchestral sound. But *Kossuth* is not only shorter in
duration than the Strauss, but rather short-winded as well; with its
ten brief sections it threatens to collapse under its own weight, but is
saved by Bartók's rather plodding, forced use of a technique of theme
transformation. The tune identified with Kossuth himself, an attempt
at Strauss's thrusting melodic manner, is altered to suit the mood and
narrative content of the different sections.

Bartók wrote the piece in piano-score first, and only orchestrated
it when a performance was assured. He wrote all his mature orchestral
works in this way as well, but was undoubtedly thinking in terms of
orchestral sound even though the appearance is that the composition
process precedes the orchestration. If he could make *Ein Heldenleben*
come to life on the piano, then his own piano writing must have been
imbued with the sound of the orchestra. Some of the instrumental
sounds Bartók later chose are unmistakably inspired by Strauss: a high
solo violin rhapsodizing in unison with a flute, and burbling
woodwind textures under a broad string theme.

The titles of the various movements come embarrassingly close
to the psychological glibness of Socialist Realism: 'What sorrow lies
so heavily on thy heart?', asks Kossuth's wife. 'Danger threatens the
fatherland', he replies. The Austrian army is heard creeping up to
a spooky suggestion of the first bars of Haydn's Austrian anthem (*Gott
erhalte*), played ominously in the minor, and the defeat of Hungary
is bemoaned in an aching funeral march that is perhaps the most
deeply-felt part of the score. The parody of the Austrian anthem, in
contrast, the most naïve aspect, brought Bartók some trouble, but
its inclusion is a good reminder of the mood of those days, when the
anthem was a loathed symbol of Austrian domination, and it was
normal for the patriotically-minded to refuse to sing it. In this spirit
Bartók wrote home more or less insisting that his little sister, Elza,
now be called by the Hungarian equivalent of her German name,
Böske. There is all sorts of evidence of his attitude: on a postcard

Bartók in 1903, around the
time of his Strauss-inspired
tone-poem *Kossuth*

Bartók scored out the bold heading *Postkarte – Carte postale* and
wrote the Hungarian instead, and he sketched a little letterhead of
the Hungarian badge on a note to his mother with the legend 'Down
with the Habsburgs!' If Paula Bartók was ever offended by this attack
on her first language, she did not make it known to her son.

In April 1903 Bartók went back to Nagyszentmiklós to give
a recital; in the aftermath, according to one Bartók biographer, Tibor
Tallián, a little romance started between the composer and Irmy, one
of the daughters of the organizer Othmár Jurkovics, a judge at the
district court. In the summer Bartók's course at the Academy came
to an end, and in June he and his fellow composition students gave
a concert of their works. Bartók's contribution, the last items on the
programme, consisted of a movement from his recent Violin Sonata,
a Fantasy for piano (dedicated to Emma Gruber), and the first movement of a sonata for the left hand. A second Fantasy was dedicated
to Irmy Jurkovics and her sister Emsy.

At the age of twenty-two Bartók's future looked promising: he had
only just graduated, but already in July 1903 a Budapest weekly music
magazine *Zenevilág* ('Music World') put a profile of him on the front
cover, predicting a great role for him in the history of Hungarian
music. He even joked with his mother that Böske should have a high
opinion of 'the future Beethoven of Hungary (!)'. He was about to

have some private piano lessons with Dohnányi, and no doubt
expected to follow him into the ranks of the leading young pianists.
Through the music salons of the city he had made numerous contacts,
and a meeting with the conductor Hans Richter, music director of
the Hallé Orchestra in Manchester, gave him the opportunity to play
Kossuth to him, on the piano. Bartók wrote to his mother describing
how much Richter was moved by the work, and how he approved of
the parody of the Austrian anthem. Richter promised to arrange for a
performance in Manchester, and in July all the arrangements were in
place for Bartók to travel to Britain. Bartók accordingly set to work
on the orchestration.

During the summer of 1903, while Bartók was in Gmunden
working with Dohnányi, the quarrel over language in the Hungarian
army, a focus for all the country's pent-up resentment, was at its
height. The Austrians refused to allow official recognition of
Hungarian in the army (and its use for commands), or to allow

Fragment of a letter written
in Gmunden in the summer
of 1903. 'I spend a lot
of time with Dohnányi ...
I showed him "Kossuth"
and he doesn't like it
very much and says it is
completely Straussian.'

Bartók and his sister Elza in 1902

the Hungarian insignia to be displayed. The customary rows over the playing in public of the Austrian anthem continued unabated.

In a letter to his mother, Bartók takes the opportunity to sound off about these topics of the day:

> *The ruin of the Hungarians will not be caused, as Dohnányi asserts, by the fact that the language and spirit of our army will be Hungarian, but much more by the fact that individual members of the Hungarian nation, with insignificant exceptions, are so distressingly indifferent to everything Hungarian.*

Further on, Bartók pompously declares:

> *All my life, in every sphere, always and in every way, I shall have one objective: the good of Hungary and the Hungarian nation.*

So the *Kossuth* symphony has to be heard in the context of these conflicts; it defines a period in Bartók's life before he departed from the national consensus, and began to side with the Hungarian avant-garde cultural movements, which were characterized by impatience with the slowness of change in Hungarian society and culture.

Bartók seems to have been actively doing the rounds during the autumn, trying to further his career by promoting himself and

making potentially useful contacts. Although he did not manage to
get in touch with Strauss, he planned to use his connection with the
Freund family to do so. Etelka Freund was a former pupil of Ferruccio
Busoni, and Bartók had given her some composition lessons earlier in
the year; her brother, a pupil of Liszt, was an acquaintance of Strauss.
Bartók played for two leading virtuosos, the violinist Fritz Kreisler
and the pianist Leopold Godowsky, and he met Busoni after a recital
he gave in Berlin in December at his own expense as part of a cam-
paign to win recognition as a concert pianist.

A German-Italian, Busoni was both a piano virtuoso and a composer, as well as an influential teacher: he taught composition in
Berlin, and piano in Weimar and Vienna. He was much more likely
to be sympathetic towards Bartók than the arrogant star of the musical world, Richard Strauss, who was not in the business of teaching
anyone. Bartók's musical interests too chimed in with Busoni's – Bach,
Beethoven and Liszt – and Bartók wrote to his mother telling her how
warmly the older man had congratulated him in his dressing room.

The trip to Berlin was followed by a performance in Vienna of
Bartók's Violin Sonata as a part of a chamber music concert by
the Fitzner Quartet, where his name appears in the august company of Haydn and Beethoven (the opus 131 quartet). In January,
in advance of the Hallé performance, *Kossuth* was heard in Budapest,
in a Philharmonic Society concert which began (ironically) with
a Haydn symphony, and included another première, a violin concerto by Jaques-Dalcroze. This was the Swiss composer and inventor
of 'Eurhythmics', whom Diaghilev and Nijinsky later visited when
they were trying to cope with choreographing the rhythmic explo-
sions of *The Rite of Spring*. Stravinsky was friendly with Jaques-
Dalcroze in his years of exile in Switzerland, and tried to interest
Diaghilev in his music.

The *Gott erhalte* parody proved a problem at rehearsals with some
players who regarded it as an act of treachery, and one trumpet player
in particular had to be persuaded to play the offending section. The
promise of scandal could only please a composer flattered by controversy, and add to popular interest in the piece. In the end the performance, conducted by István Kerner, in the leading concert hall in the
city, the Vigadó, was a success. It suggests something of a confusion
in the minds of the Budapest audience that it was ready to applaud

a symphonic poem with an overtly nationalist programme, despite being in the very latest German style. If it is worth hearing now, quite apart from throwing an intriguing light on the composer's early development, it is because of its very fashionableness to the audience of the day. With its topical subject, it is the musical counterpart to the historical paintings which adorn the Budapest Parliament. At the end of the evening, Bartók's name was made, and when the reviews appeared he found himself propelled to the front rank of Hungarian composers.

Richter kept his promise, and Bartók travelled to Manchester for the second performance of the symphonic poem, which was given on 18 February. He stayed at the Richter family home, where he got on particularly well with the youngest girl in the family, Thildi. He also appeared as a performer in the concert, playing Liszt's *Rhapsodie Espagnole* (orchestrated by Busoni) and a set of variations on a theme by Handel by the Hungarian composer Robert Volkmann. The British press heard the Strauss connection in *Kossuth* immediately, and commented on the naïvety of the parody. After this less than total success, Richter's attitude to Bartók became increasingly luke-warm. In the meantime Dohnányi, who was also in touch with Richter, helped to get Bartók a recital for the Broadwood Ladies' Concerts. As Malcolm Gillies points out in his detailed study of Bartók's connections with Britain, this was particularly useful since Bartók received no payment for the Hallé concert.

In 1904 his work appeared in print for the first time when the Budapest publisher Bárd contacted him. They were possibly prompted to do so by the success of *Kossuth*, but there was no attempt to publish that piece. Instead they brought out two collections of other existing work; one of four piano pieces, including the Fantasy Bartók had played at his graduation recital, and the other of four songs on texts by Lajos Pósa.

Bartók spent a large part of the year in the rural Slovakian resort of Gerlicepuszta (now Ratkó), which he made his base until late in the autumn. While he was there, continuing to compose in his established manner, he had a musical experience that he was quite unprepared for, one which changed the course of his life.

Bartók had gone alone to the resort, to devote his time to prepar-ing for a concert in Budapest scheduled for the following spring.

Lidi Dósa, c. 1904, whose singing first alerted Bartók to the hidden treasure of Hungarian folk-song.

Opposite, Bartók's first works in print were these Four Songs on texts by Lajos Pósa; his cousin Ervin Voit designed the cover.

He was going to perform a new work of his own, a Scherzo for piano and orchestra, and Liszt's *Totentanz*, so he shut himself away to practise the Liszt and orchestrate the Scherzo. There was a Budapest family staying in the same building and with them was their servant, Lidi Dósa, a Székely Hungarian from Transylvania. Bartók heard her singing a simple song to a child: 'A red apple fell down into the mud/Whoever picks it up won't do so in vain'. Intrigued, he asked her to sing any other old village songs she might know, learned from her grandmother. Rather like any classical musician in Europe with an interest in folklore, Bartók afterwards made a simple arrangement of *Piros alma* ('Red apple') and this was published the next year in the magazine *Magyar Lant* ('Hungarian Lute').

However banal this response may have been, Bartók had certainly made an important discovery. Lidi Dósa had given a member of the educated Hungarian middle class his first experience of Hungarian folk music, a culture he knew nothing about. For all Bartók's trumpetings of patriotism over the previous year, he was aware of no Hungarian music he could feel sufficiently proud of. Then he heard *Piros alma*. Of course the implications were not immediately apparent: a composer filled with the spirit of Liszt and Richard Strauss, eager to write vast, noisy orchestral works, and to make his way on the international piano circuit was unlikely to see the future in this unadorned single line of melody. But a seed was planted that was to bear much more lasting fruit than any of Bartók's other activities and interests in his first few years as a professional musician.

In November Bartók went back to Pozsony and gave his first recital there, with a programme heavily weighted towards Liszt. The last item, the Third Mephisto Waltz, has great resonance in Bartók's own work: a *danse macabre* derived from Berlioz and Liszt is a persistent feature of Bartók's music up to the 1920s. A Rhapsody for piano which he wrote during this summer (opus 1 of his latest and last listing) reflects another Lisztian manner, that of the Hungarian Rhapsodies. Clearly a full awareness of what was genuinely Hungarian was still to come.

After a couple of months at home. Bartók moved to Vienna in the new year, and he stayed there until May. He returned to Budapest only to take part in the concert at which he played Liszt's *Totentanz*, and while he scored a great success with this, the planned perform-

ance of the Scherzo for piano and orchestra did not go ahead. The orchestral musicians claimed that it could not be played.

In Vienna he was composing a five-movement suite for orchestra, a confident, almost brash piece of turn-of-the-century music, but one which has great breadth (the composer was only just twenty-four) and passion. There is little that is original in the mixture of Liszt and Strauss allied to a *csárdás* idiom, and the Vienna performance at a concert of premières in November brought the composer quite a success. That this was a nationalist victory for Bartók is expressed in an autobiographical note he wrote for a programme at a recital in Sopron: 'A week ago my orchestral suite, in all its Hungarian-ness, caused a sensation *in Vienna*.'

In July 1905 Bartók set off for Paris, for what should have been the climax to his run of triumphs: the Rubinstein Competition, which he entered both as performer and composer. He had no success in either category; the setback took the wind out of his sails, and the cockiness of the First Suite never surfaced again. The Rubinstein jury gave the piano prize to Wilhelm Backhaus, but withheld the composition prize. Bartók's feelings about this are expressed in a letter to his mother:

I'm not in the least surprised that I didn't win a prize as a pianist, and there's no need to feel disappointed on that score. But the way in which the prizes for composers were distributed – or rather not distributed – that was quite outrageous.

Bartók entered his *Concertstück* arrangement (for piano and orchestra) of the Rhapsody, and his Piano Quintet. The latter was turned down by the panel on the grounds that there was no time for players to learn it, and Bartók quickly substituted the Violin Sonata of 1903. He had a struggle to have the *Concertstück* accepted, but in the end it was the work of an Italian entrant, Brugnoli, which got the first mention (but not a prize). Bartók's rage against the iniquities of the voting arrangements and the wasted effort of making a second copy of the Quintet is understandable, but such are the attendant risks of a composers' competition. Nevertheless Bartók's view of his own worth was not shaken: 'I must say that Brugnoli's pieces are absolutely worthless conglomerations. It is quite scandalous that the jury could not see how much better my works are'.

Following page, Elizabeth Bridge, Budapest, looking towards Pest. Built during Bartók's first years in the city, at the time of its completion in 1903 it was the largest single-span bridge in Europe.

Zoltán Kodály, Bartók's lifelong friend and confidant;
'His greatest quality was
his presence ... a strong,
radiating force' (Antal Doráti)

Bartók was still in correspondence with Irmy Jurkovics in
Nagyszentmiklós, and a long letter to her records his impressions of
Paris, his current feelings about art in general and Hungarian culture
and society, and his first declaration that he is a 'follower of
Nietzsche'. He was clearly entranced by Paris ('this heavenly godless
city'), its museums and parks, and enthused about the Murillos he
saw in the Louvre. Still he maintains the superiority of Austro-
German music (his 'big four' are Bach, Beethoven, Schubert and
Wagner), but he is now aware of the importance of Hungarian folk
music, 'vastly superior' to that of other nations. For the first time
he is sure that the future of Hungary lies in the education of the

provinces. He also shared his thoughts on religion, opening a discussion on the subject: 'It is odd that the Bible says, "God created man", whereas it is the other way round: man has created God.' Overall, this long letter finds him trying to rationalize and rise above the depression which he fell into after his complete failure in the competition. The following month, while he was still in Paris, he wrote to his mother that Mihalovich was trying to create a teaching post for him at the Academy; by now he was resigned to taking the first post that came along.

He returned to Vienna in October with little to look forward to, no concerts to perform in, and with his composing once again halted. Various letters show that he was full of anger against the status quo: the urban culture of Budapest, organized religion, the social position of women. There are even anti-Semitic comments, which may have been inspired by a sense of loneliness and of being an outsider, or perhaps simply in imitation of the Arányis, who despite being Jewish themselves were not averse to this kind of sentiment.

In March 1906 Emma Gruber introduced him to the man who was to become his firmest friend and ally, Zoltán Kodály. Kodály was only a year younger than Bartók, and had been studying composition at the Academy of Music (also with Koessler) at the same time. He had combined this with a degree in German and Hungarian literature at the University, and went straight on to take a Ph.D. on the stanza structure of Hungarian folk-song. Kodály's education was rather different from Bartók's: he was much less self-taught and much less

Bartók photographed in Spain in 1906, during his tour accompanying the violinist Ferenc Vecsey

a trainee professional musician. The fact that Bartók, in all other relationships so reserved and quietly self-possessed, was open to all musical suggestions Kodály might make, is not explained simply by Kodály's firmer academic background. Tall and thin, with his red beard and piercing eyes, Kodály had the look of a Greek saint. The Hungarian conductor Antal Doráti, a pupil of Kodály's in the 1920s, remembers him as a Christ-like figure with a radiant presence. The pursuit of folk-song was the two men's original point of contact, but they soon began to develop as composers together, Kodály influencing Bartók's decision-making all the time.

Kodály's studies were based on the field recordings of Hungarian material which the anthropologist (and musically illiterate) Béla Vikár had started making in 1898 with an Edison phonograph. Like earlier folklorists, Vikár was primarily concerned with the texts of the songs, not the music. Kodály had only just started collecting in the field himself, and Bartók was to follow suit in the summer of 1906. His sister was by now married to a landowner in Vésztő, in Békés County, on the great plain near the present border with Romania. Bartók left from here on his first field excursions, using local, educated contacts to find informants, farm workers, shepherds, swineherds, whom he recorded on wax cylinders. It must have been strange for Bartók, who had spent his childhood in the Hungarian provinces, to encounter another world which had been there all the time while he was growing up, hidden from him behind the invisible wall of his social status and culture.

Bartók had visited Spain and Portugal in the spring of 1906, as the accompanist of the thirteen-year-old violin virtuoso Ferenc Vecsey, already famous and the dedicatee of Sibelius's (revised) Violin Concerto. This was his last such concert tour for many years, and the child prodigy Vecsey was the star attraction, not Bartók. Vecsey's father accompanied the two musicians on the trip, and Bartók remembered him in scathing terms years later in a letter to another violin virtuoso, József Szigeti. Mr Vecsey, on discovering that the elderly French composer Saint-Saëns was in Oporto, arranged for his son to play for him. Saint-Saëns had listened, corrected a mistaken tempo and left. Mr Vecsey's reaction was 'Oh, he does not understand, he is not a violinist'.

Opposite, Bartók dressed for the countryside, Csík County, 1907

In the summer Bartók returned to collecting folk material in the countryside. He and Kodály were now working as a team, and the two men set out individually, on separate routes, in a spirit that combined nationalism with back-to-nature asceticism. The result of their journeys was a publication, *Magyar Népdalok* ('Hungarian Folk-Songs'), paid for by the two men and a handful of subscribers, of twenty song arrangements for voice and piano (ten by each composer). Sales were minimal, and only thirty years later did the first print-run sell out.

While pursuing his new interest, Bartók took pride in turning up at the Vecsey family home on the outskirts of Budapest in his guise of anarchic folklorist and drop-out, upsetting the rigid etiquette of the household. He wrote to his aunt Irma:

As I have a taste for dissonance, I intend to invade this scene of awful orderliness wearing my summer shirt, without collar or cuffs, and my oldest shoes – just to shock them!

Bartók had found his spiritual home in the countryside, and had begun to immerse himself in the culture and music of the peasants with the same enthusiasm he had shown for Strauss.

3

Design by the architect
Károly Kós for the church
of Zebegény, 1908. His
researches into folk art
mirrored those of Bartók
and Kodály in music.

*After reading your letter, I sat down at the
piano – I have sad misgivings that I shall never
find any consolation in life save in music.*

Bartók to Stefi Geyer, September 1907

Portrait of a Girl 1907–9

At the beginning of 1907 Mihalovich suddenly got his chance to help Bartók when Thomán decided to stand down from teaching at the Academy. The Director immediately appointed Bartók to the piano-teaching staff to fill the gap. Thomán was still only in his forties when he left the staff, and he remained in contact with his former pupil for many years; more than thirty years later Bartók played in a seventy-fifth-birthday concert for him. But while Thomán had held an important post on the Academy staff, Bartók, who assumed the title of Professor on 17 January, was never a head of department. When he joined the piano staff at the age of twenty-five, the heads were Árpád Szendy for the performer's diploma and Chován for the teacher's. In accepting the job it is likely that Bartók started to find a new stability and focus after the indecisive last few years. It was becoming apparent that a career as a solo pianist was not going to take off, and as for composing, he had written no new music since beginning a second orchestral suite immediately after finishing the first, two years before.

The Academy of Music (later the Liszt Academy) in Budapest, where Bartók spent his entire teaching career

Aladár Kriesch: *The Fountain of Art*, from the Academy interior, 1907

In the same year that Bartók started to teach there, the Academy moved from its old premises on Andrássy út to a brand-new building on Liszt Ferenc tér. The building was constructed according to the conventional plan of music academies throughout Europe, with a concert hall (complete with organ) at its centre, accessible from the ground and first floors; administrative offices were situated in the surrounding corridors and teaching rooms were on the floors above. The acoustic of the concert hall would later be described by Stravinsky as one of the best in the world.

The new Academy building was a splendid example of the current Hungarian flowering of Art Nouveau. The interior decoration is still a surprise: the stained glass and squat columns of turquoise and gold are more reminiscent of an early cinema or turn-of-the-century fairground than an educational establishment. The most striking elements are the wall-painting of the chaste nudes bathing in the waters of 'The Fountain of Art' and the frieze 'Hungarian Wedding Procession in the Fourteenth Century' by one of the architects of the building, Aladár Kriesch.

In the deadpan style of his 1921 autobiographical note Bartók crystallizes the significance of the Academy post in a few neat phrases:

Left, Budapest Post Office Savings Bank, 1900. The architect, Ödön Lechner, was a pioneer of the Hungarian style of Art Nouveau architecture.

'I particularly welcomed this appointment because it gave me an opportunity to settle down at home and pursue my research into folk music'. It also kept him in day-to-day contact with his new mentor, Kodály, who had recently been made a Professor of Composition at the Academy. Bartók considered him his only friend there, and students remember that when the two men were teaching in adjoining classrooms they would confer in the connecting 'professor's anteroom', Kodály quietly expounding words of wisdom which Bartók absorbed in silence. Apart from the chaotic period of the 1918–19 revolutions, when, like every other institution in the country, the Academy saw three changes of direction, Bartók kept himself apart from the rest of the staff and administration. He had a direct influence on generations of Hungarian music students, but, as they all testify, he taught simply by example, just as he had been taught.

Ernő Balogh was a pupil of Bartók's when he first began to teach, and he had reasonably warm memories of the classes:

All of his students admired and loved him for his genius, of which we were convinced, for his profound knowledge of every phrase in music, for his gentle and kind manners, for his unfailing logic, for his convincing explanation of every detail. He was just and fair, but could not conceal his annoyance with his less gifted students.

The essence of his approach was that he taught music first and piano second. Immaculate musicianship was the most important part of his guidance and influence … He had unlimited patience to explain details of phrasing, rhythm, touch, pedalling. He was unforgiving for the tiniest deviation or sloppiness in rhythm … Bartók insisted on first solving the musical problems and then the pianistic ones. In fact, he was not deeply interested in pianistic problems. He had a natural technique and although he was recognized in time as a virtuoso, virtuoso problems did not interest him.

The years spent in a job he did not enjoy apparently had an increasingly detrimental effect on the classroom atmosphere. The writer Julia Székely studied with Bartók some years later, in the 1920s, and she left this rather forbidding recollection of piano classes with him in her book *Professor Bartók*:

*When the student brought a newly-learnt piece to the lesson for the
first time, he sat at the writing desk and heard it through without
interruptions … After he had heard the piece right through he got up
from the writing desk and sat down at the second piano. He did not say
a word, and left the student without any idea of whether he had performed well or poorly.*

In these first months of full-time employment Bartók continued
to lodge with the Vecsey family, but in May Paula Bartók moved
up from Pozsony, and she and her son rented a house in the Pest
suburb of Rákospalota for the summer. It was only in the autumn
that they moved to a flat right in the heart of the city, at 17 Teréz
körút, a few minutes' walk away from the Academy, and here they
stayed until 1911.

Even at this early stage Bartók was clearly overcoming the
entrenched nationalism of his fellow-Hungarians (and moving far
away from his own earlier nationalist enthusiasm) and widening the
scope of his folk-music research to include the music of the ethnic
minorities within Hungary. Throughout the country Slovaks and
Romanians were regarded with particular mistrust by ethnic
Hungarians, but Bartók had no such prejudices, and he would later
be attacked repeatedly in the press for his refusal to go along with
popular sentiment. Bartók invoked the precept of scientific
comparison to justify the broadening scope of his research, and
indeed the developing discipline of ethnomusicology was quick to
employ scientific terminology. Its first practitioners were generally
scientists first and musicians second. An area of such ethnic diversity
as Hungary before World War I was ideal for comparing
different musical traditions.

For some time artists and architects had been collecting folk
artefacts and finding an inspiration in vernacular architectural styles.
Like Bartók and Kodály, they were inspired by the traditions of the
Hungarian countryside. A leading architect of this school was Károly
Kós, who designed mostly private homes, although he built a few
public buildings, including churches, in the folk-influenced style.
Transylvania was the favoured destination for the artists' field trips,
and it was natural that Bartók would want to travel there too. He
was hoping to find forms of Hungarian song that had died out

Above, 'Matyo Peasants',
lithograph by István Zichy,
1908, a leading figure in
the group of Art Nouveau
artists who founded an
Arts and Crafts colony at
Gödöllő, north of Budapest
Left, design for a hall
window in 'Lapis Refugii',
a fantasy house, by
Lajos Kozma

Design for the yard of
a manor house, by
Károly Kós, printed in
the influential periodical
Magyar Iparmüvészet
('Hungarian Applied Arts')
in 1908

Bartók recording folk-
song in 1907, in Daraz,
Nyitra County, now
Drazovce, Slovakia

elsewhere, among the Székely people, whose culture had developed
in isolation from the Hungarian mainstream. Lidi Dósa, his first
informant, was herself a Székely.

No academy of music in Europe would at this time have had any
interest in folk music as a serious topic of study for talented musicians; the Budapest Academy was no exception, and little financial
help could be expected. But two years before, in 1905, Bartók had
had an application for a grant to finance a research trip approved by
a government ministry (Religion and Public Education). It is possible
that the destination was a deciding factor in the grant being supplied.
Transylvania was a disputed area, and with its large Romanian
population, it had long been a focus for 'Magyarization'; it would

eventually be ceded to Romania after World War I. Bartók collected his grant and in the summer of 1907 set off with his wax cylinders to record the music which was now as important to him as the classics of the learned European tradition.

One of the first things Bartók did when he arrived in Transylvania was to have some traditional furniture made by a carpenter in Körösfő (now Crişeni, in Romania). Photographs from the following year show the furniture – a writing desk, table, chairs – installed in the Teréz körút flat, and the same furniture can still be seen in the

Right, Peasant furniture and, *below,* Bartók playing a hurdy-gurdy (*nyenyere*) in his Teréz körút flat, June 1908

Budapest Bartók-House, although the painted roses which Bartók
describes on his cabinets have faded. Perhaps he wanted to recreate
in the heart of the city some of the peace and simplicity of his
summers in the country. He had a similar intention in mind for the
musical material he was collecting. On the one hand there was the
scholarly aspect of listing and comparing, and the desire to preserve
what was disappearing under the effects of industrialization. But the
folk-songs had a purely musical value as well: they were material for
Bartók the composer, and, intriguingly, an enthusiastic message to
Etelka Freund on a picture postcard from Transylvania sent in August
puts both themes together: the fact that he has discovered examples
of tunes which he had thought were lost, and that the fourth movement of his Second Orchestral Suite is waiting to be orchestrated.
The revelations of folk music were inspiring the composer to start
writing again.

It was possibly during his first half-year as a teacher that Bartók
came into contact with a nineteen-year old girl, Stefi Geyer, who was

Stefi Geyer in 1905,
dedicatee and inspiration of
Bartók's First Violin Concerto

studying violin at the Academy under Jenő Hubay. Certainly he was with her and her brother in June 1907, just before the Transylvanian trip, in Jászberény, a town east of Budapest, on the edge of the Great Plain. Stefi may not have given him much encouragement, but she became the focus of his romantic passion, the recipient of his most personal thoughts and the dedicatee and protagonist of much of the music that he began to write later in 1907. Bartók's few letters to her are the only existing statements of belief and purpose the composer made, but their overt seriousness can seem too well organized for there to be anything unwittingly revealing. The letters also come so early in Bartók's life that they can be no more than a starting-point for an understanding of the mature man.

The first of his published letters to her is dated 16 August, the day before his card to Etelka Freund. This is a long, light-hearted, if rather wry depiction of the difficulties of folk-song collecting, written as a dialogue between researcher and informants. Three weeks later Bartók had left Transylvania and was staying once again with Böske and her family in Vésztő. The immensely long letter from this address, written perhaps after everyone has gone to bed ('It is one o'clock in the morning'), covers in detail Bartók's reasons for his atheism, as well as what he views as his purpose in life. Perhaps Stefi was prodding him with little malicious darts to have prompted this avalanche. Bartók has passed beyond the Nietzschean sentiments expressed earlier and embraced greater tolerance: 'let everyone do as he likes, it's no business of mine.' He expresses a faith in nature and science, and sees atheism as the natural successor to Christianity ('distorted into Catholicism'), which in turn ('with its splendid code of ethics') had taken over from the faiths of the ancient world. The world view retains something of his Christian upbringing: 'everybody and every living thing – even mosquitoes and fleas – has an object in life'. He then describes his own object: 'on however small a scale to give a few minor pleasures; on a bigger scale, to work for the good of that set of corrupt demi-gentlemen we call the Hungarian intelligentsia by collecting folk-songs, etc. etc.' Apparently the Trinity is what concerns Stefi, but Bartók declares that if he ever crossed himself, it would be 'in the name of Nature, Art and Science'.

Her reply to this is still unpublished, but Bartók's following letter gives an idea of what it contained.

I anticipated you might react like this, yet when you actually did so, I was upset. Why couldn't I read your letter with cold indifference? Why couldn't I put it down with a smile of contempt? … Or maybe I am after all mistaken in thinking that you accept as true that clumsy fable about the Holy Trinity?

Of course there was nothing unusual at this time about an atheist philosophy for educated people of Bartók's generation and background, but in Hungary this generation was starting to reject the conservative nationalism of the establishment as well. Possibly the dialogue with Stefi finds Bartók defining his outlook not merely for her or himself, but in the wider context of Hungarian cultural life. What is unmistakable from the letters is that Bartók was deeply in love with this girl, and the failure of the relationship to develop plunged him into a period of great bleakness.

Wrapped up in his love for this (unattainable) girl, Bartók gave her two exalted roles to play. One was the intellectual correspondent and confidante, and the other was his muse. She inspired, or was used to inspire the span of music which saw him gradually finding his feet as an original composer. The first problem he had to face, and it was a fundamental problem for any composer of Bartók's generation, was the choice of musical idiom to adopt. He had sailed through the confident excess of the Straussian tone-poem in *Kossuth* and the First Orchestral Suite. Then for two years he had been unable to make any progress until his enthusiasm for folk-music had rekindled his instinct to compose. If he was immediately aware of the basic contradiction implicit in any attempt to reconcile the musical elaborations of the Austro-German tradition with folk source material, then the naïve way a pentatonic (five-note) theme is used in the last movement of the Second Orchestral Suite does not show it. The orchestral colouring and the way the harmony is used to build up to powerful climaxes is still recognizably drawn from Strauss, and the effect is almost as incongruous as peasant furniture in a city-centre flat. A more promising start is the more conventional, but more purely imaginative third movement: unambiguously subtitled *Scena della puszta* ('Scene of the plain') when the whole work was revised years later, this is a calm evocation of the Hungarian plain which opens with an elaborate, meandering yet self-possessed bass-clarinet melody.

The composers of Bartók's generation had moved away from the nationalism of those late-nineteenth century composers, Smetana, Grieg, Dvořák, who had created a local dialect of the Austro-German language. An alternative was hard to find, especially in an art-form still dominated by the German tradition, and at this stage Bartók had yet to come into contact with the music of Mussorgsky, the most assuredly primitive of Russia's folk-inspired composers, and the most independent from Western European traditions. Mussorgsky's music, with its home-made technique and earthy sound, was one of the springboards for Debussy's leap away from the academic certainties taught in the Paris Conservatoire (although the young Debussy did not hear it, as has been claimed, when employed by the family of Tchaikovsky's patron, Nadezhda von Meck). Bartók was still leaning towards the Austro-German school he had been brought up with, while Kodály came back from a long visit to Paris, in their first full year as colleagues at the Academy, filled with enthusiasm for Debussy.

Bartók intuitively recognized the roots of the French composer's new, subjective approach to harmony; it chimed in with what he had experienced 'in the field', and what he had already created in the final chord of his *Scena della puszta* – not constructed according to the 'rules' of harmony, but simply made, in his words, 'by the simultaneous sounding of the notes of the much repeated motive'. To understand the progressive nature of such a cavalier approach to harmony, it should be remembered that only a few years before Schoenberg's string sextet *Verklärte Nacht* had been refused performance because it contained a chord which could not be justified in terms of conventional harmony.

Bartók had one last Austro-German influence to work out, and this he did in the context of two pieces specifically addressed to Stefi. There are many conventional aspects to Bartók's work throughout his life: even in his most forward-looking piano music he continues, with subtitles, dedications and cryptic messages, the tradition of Romantic music, the *morceaux de salon*, and the furious, Lisztian virtuoso display piece. The experience of his faltering affair with Stefi called up just such a conventional response: he dedicated a violin concerto to her. In his second long letter to Stefi, he assigns her a yearning, Wagnerian theme ('This is your Leitmotiv'), in the context of a rich, Romantic Adagio, with, in one place, the thudding rhythm of a funeral march.

Bartók had already begun the concerto which opens with this Stefi theme, and he worked on it during the winter of 1907–8. For the first time he used the two-movement structure (Slow–Fast) which, borrowed from the *verbunkos*, would remain a characteristic of his work. Stefi understood not only what was intended, that the first movement depicted herself, 'the young girl whom he loved, the second the violinist whom he admired', but also what was the composer's authentic voice. Perceptively, she wrote that the first movement was less Bartók than the second, and indeed the serene opening movement shows that Bartók has been looking at the mixture of contrapuntal textures and late-Romantic harmony that characterizes the somewhat grandiose music of the German composer Max Reger. He visited the composer in Leipzig that very summer before writing the concerto.

The second movement is quite different, a virtuoso display, still playing with the Stefi theme, but in a much lighter mood. Bartók wrote that he intended this to portray the witty, entertaining side to Stefi's personality. The quotation of a German folk-song (accompanied by plodding harp chords – a frequently used effect) is marked in the manuscript 'Jászberény, 28 June 1907', in memory of the happy times of the previous summer, and perhaps the moment when he fell in love with Stefi. He finished the concerto on 5 February 1908, and sent Stefi the score (accompanied by a Béla Balázs poem); just eight days later she wrote to him breaking off a relationship which was more imagined than real. Bartók tore out the dedication to her and the concerto was never performed in his (or Stefi's) lifetime. It is interesting that it is the well-composed, if less original movement that Bartók retained, and resurrected some time later, first with one companion piece, then with another. For the moment, however, he chose to express his blighted love in musical terms, in a string quartet.

At this time Bartók was composing music without any guarantee of performance, genuinely 'for his desk'. Composers of new music in Hungary were having the same difficulties as elsewhere in Europe, in terms of audience reception, but Hungary in the first decade of the century was experiencing a wider political and cultural crisis that provides the special context for Bartók's musical development. In politics the opposing ranks were drawing up on the right and left, and in the arts the pressure to salute the flag of the national-liberal

Opposite, autograph of the second movement of the 'Stefi' Violin Concerto, showing the quotation of a song 'Der Esel ist ein dummes Tier' (The donkey is a stupid beast).

Title page of the first edition of *For Children*, Bartók's four-volume collection of folk-based piano pieces, 1910

consensus was being openly rejected. As early as 1896 there had been
a reaction to the accepted styles in the visual arts – heroic history
painting on one hand, and narrative realism on the other. Artists, and
soon writers and musicians, were not only looking objectively at the
country's cultural inheritance, but turning their sights westwards to
the decadent artists of Paris. Kodály's enthusiasm for Debussy falls
into the same pattern. The journal *Nyugat* ('West') crystallizes this
new strain, and Bartók's music was already a topic of discussion in
an article in its first edition, in 1908. The author of the article, Géza
Csáth, doctor, opium-addict and author of nasty tales, would have

heard only *Kossuth* and some of the First Suite, both by now unrep-
resentative of Bartók's work, but he stressed the composer's folk music
inspiration, and in all the article served to connect Bartók's name with
the new artistic movements.

Bartók worked on the String Quartet for a year, and the piece must
have been affected by the sudden great burst of creativity, especially
in writing for the piano, that occurred at this time. His compositions
in this period up to 1911 cannot easily be organized in terms of a line
of development, and the opus numbers are not a reliable indication
of what was composed when.

At the age of twenty-six, Bartók had his first folk music article
published when the fruits of the previous summer's Transylvanian
field trip appeared in *Ethnographia*, the journal of the Hungarian
Ethnographic Society. Around the same time he was asked to pre-
pare an edition of Bach's *Well-Tempered Clavier* for teaching purposes,
by the Budapest music publisher Rozsnyai (whose first connection
with Bartók had been through the publication of the Twenty
Hungarian Folk-songs), and the edition appeared a few months afterwards. Curiously the Forty-Eight Preludes and Fugues are rearranged
in order of difficulty, not, as written, according to Bach's key scheme.

There was also a commission from the same publisher for some
original teaching music, and this inspired the four volumes of
Gyermekeknek ('For Children'). These pieces mark the beginnings of
Bartók's folk-piano manner, and consist of simple arrangements for

Title page of the first edition
of *Two Portraits*, 1911, in
which Bartók re-used the
first movement of his suppressed 'Stefi' concerto

BÉLA·BARTÓK

OP. 5.

DEUX·PORTRAITS
POUR·ORCHESTRE

CHARLES·ROZSNYAI
EDITEUR·BUDAPEST.

piano of folk melodies, with the most unobtrusive harmonies, made during 1908 and 1909. A more personal note is struck in the Fourteen Bagatelles and Ten Easy Pieces which were composed together during May and June 1908. Stefi, in the familiar guise of her rising four-note theme, makes an appearance as the unnamed subject of the 'Dedication' that precedes the ten pieces. More grotesquely, she is the focus of the last two bagatelles: 'Elle est morte –', dominated by the thudding funeral-march rhythm, and the following 'Ma mie qui danse', a whirling dance piece that echoes the spirit of Berlioz and Liszt. Just to make the point of No. 13 utterly clear, Bartók wrote 'She is dead' at the point where Stefi's theme appears in the last five bars. It was the last Bagatelle which finally provided him with the solution for his unperformed concerto. In a squealing orchestral version, he tacked it on to the serene first movement to create *Two Portraits* (One ideal, one grotesque). The work carries the opus number 5, but this is no guide to when he actually constructed it: the Bagatelles, after all, are opus 6.

The *For Children* pieces provided Bartók with just the right dis-cipline for rethinking the harmonization of folk melodies, and com-plementing this, the Bagatelles gave him an outlet for all his most progressive ideas. In the few short years since emulating the right-up-to-date Richard Strauss, the rate of change in modern music had speeded up alarmingly. Western music was then, if not now, inex-tricably linked to an idea of evolution – throughout Bartók's lifetime Beethoven was seen as a progression from, not to mention improve-ment on Mozart – and Bartók the ethnographer as much as the composer would have subscribed to the view that music 'developed' from primitive material into increasingly complex structures.

However, a break with the certainties of the past was becoming more evident with every passing year of the new century. Principles so long-established that they were taken to be self-evident were being questioned and rejected. The idea was current that the blurring of harmony in the works of Wagner and the late-Romantic composers had destroyed the need for those pillars of musical construction, major and minor keys. An analogy might be found in painting, where first traditional subject-matter, then perspective and finally natural representation were gradually abandoned. In music there was as yet no international agreement on where the future lay, and composers

Opposite, Hungarian title page of the first edition of Ten Easy Pieces, 1908. A German title page was also prepared for the same edition.

EIGENTUM DES VERLEGERS FÜR ALLE LÄNDER

KARL ROZSNYAI
BUCH- UND MUSIKALIENVERLAGSHANDLUNG
BUDAPEST
IV MÚZEUM KÖRÚT 15.

R.K.293.sz.

Lith.Anst.v.C.G.Roder G.m.b.H.,Leipzig.Budapest IX.

were feeling their way forward note by note. At precisely this time
Schoenberg was arriving at his concept of 'the emancipation of the
dissonance', a theory that all notes were equal. The Fourteen
Bagatelles are Bartók's personal thoughts on the new possibilities,
and some of his experiments are startlingly original. Key signatures
appear only in the first piece, and then, provocatively, Bartók gives
a different one to each of the two musical lines – in piano terms, one
key signature for the right hand, and another one for the left.

Two folk tunes are used in the collection, and identified as Slovak
and Hungarian, with the words underlaid. What sort of pieces are
these then? Are they songs, or are the words a message to the performer alone? One is harmonized with plodding, Mussorgskian
chords, the other with rapidly repeated clumps of notes, chosen to
freeze the sense of changing harmony. Like a poet in a flash of
inspiration finding words and images that conceal from the reader
the absence of rhyme or metre, Bartók chooses sounds that we
intuitively hear as right. The collection still follows the conventions
of Romantic piano music – the very title indicates as much, but these
are exciting and rewarding pieces at the forefront of the avant garde.

While Bartók was completing all this piano music, the String
Quartet was still progressing. There are signs that a change is taking
place in the composer and his outlook in the way this asymmetric
work is shaped, and how it gradually develops from a bleak opening
movement, still tied to Austro-German Romanticism, to an ebullient
dance, inspired by, rather than quoting folk music. Indeed, the last
movement of the Quartet is the first example of the familiar Bartók
dance finale, and it marks the first appearance of his unmistakable
wild and driving string idiom.

When Stefi ended any hope for Bartók that his love might be
returned (and in doing so, according to Kodály, brought Bartók 'to
the verge of non-existence'), the composer comforted himself by
spending the summer travelling. He first visited Busoni in Vienna,
and a postcard to Etelka Freund records that the older composer 'was
very pleased with the piano pieces.' 'Endlich etwas wirklich neues'
[at last something really new], he said. Bartók played the whole set
the following day for Busoni's piano class, Busoni recommended the
pieces to his own publisher, Breitkopf and Härtel. They turned them
down, however, considering them too modern and too difficult;

Rozsnyai, now Bartók's regular Budapest publisher, accepted the
pieces the following year.

Bartók then went on through Switzerland ('over-civilized') and into
France, apparently travelling only in the company of his Baedeker.
This solitary way of life came to an end with the autumn term. In
September 1908 two sisters, Herma and Márta Ziegler, became private
pupils of Bartók. Márta was only fifteen, twelve years younger than
Béla, but a straightforward loving relationship developed rapidly
between teacher and pupil. In the case of Márta there is no trace of
any letters like those to Stefi, and her role as muse was a much more
realistic one. How did Bartók relate to women at this time? His
mother never ceased to be utterly devoted to him, and even from
photographs of the two together it is clear that the adoration was
mutual. At this time his mother was still looking after him in his city
flat, and this continuation of the home environment of his childhood
perhaps left him too immature for the self-possessed Stefi. Possibly,
despite the twelve-year difference, he and Márta had reached the same
level of emotional maturity when they first met.

Almost immediately Bartók made a musical sketch of Márta in
'Portrait of a Girl', for piano. This became the first of Seven Sketches,
put together over the following two years, while other music was
being worked on. The contrast with the Stefi music – first exalted,
then despairing – is striking. By all accounts Márta was a sweet, good-
natured girl, and the piece, with its brief, easy-going phrases confirms
that description. Bartók the Romantic cannot resist an autobiographical touch at the end, though: Stefi's motif, upside-down, is the final,
seemingly inconsequential phrase of the piece.

Bartók was soon commemorating the experiences they shared in
music. One evening late in November they had a quarrel: the first of
Three Burlesques for piano says as much in the published title. An
unpublished title is more specific; in a mixture of languages it reads,
*Rage over an interrupted visit/or/Rondoletto a capriccio/ or/Revenge is
sweet/or/Play it if you can/or/November 27/Please choose from these titles!*
Like the Sketches, the collection of Burlesques was completed over
a number of years, and the two sets were published by Rozsnyai in
1911 and 1912 respectively. Another sketch was added the following
February, and Bartók made a copy for Márta in the shape of a spiral,
using a special nib to draw the staves. Again there is a private title as

Title page of the first edition
of Three Burlesques (1912),
the most striking of Ervin
Voit's designs

well as the published one of 'See-saw, Dickory-daw': 'In memory of 6,
7, 8, 9, 10, 11 pm, 16 Feb 1909'. These autobiographical pieces conjure
up a mood of cosy physical intimacy far removed from the unrequited
passion of the previous year.

Bartók's new music, almost all for piano, was not reaching a wide
audience either within Hungary or anywhere else in Europe. While
his contemporaries in Vienna were already causing controversy, the
only comparable event for Bartók was the performance of an orchestral piece – one movement from the Second Suite – in Berlin in
January 1909, which Busoni set up for him. Busoni also seems to
have flattered him into conducting the orchestra himself, and Bartók
suspected, probably correctly, that the offer was made only because
someone else had dropped out. The audience was split into two
opposing camps, with Busoni's supporters taking Bartók's side, and
a noisy battle erupted at the end of the piece. Bartók had earned his
spurs as a demon of the avant garde with a work which, he wrote, 'is
really not bad', but which embodied an idiom he was leaving behind.

During 1909 Bartók was brought face to face with the difficulties involved in having works performed in Budapest. The fact the performances went ahead at all was an improvement on the previous year, when the Academy orchestra refused to play the Second Suite, and the conductor's sudden indisposition meant the cancellation of a performance of the first. These were the works, along with the opus 1 Rhapsody for piano and orchestra, which roused the conservative musical establishment to invective against the composer. There is really nothing in these rather derivative, if noisy and prolix works to justify such a reaction. A more likely explanation lies in Bartók's association with the *Nyugat* circle, even if that was only an association in print. Almost immediately a conservative journal, the *Magyar Figyelő* ('Hungarian Observer'), had been brought out in response to *Nyugat*, which thundered against radical writers' desire to 'ruin our morals, disillusion us of our faith, and crush our national pride.'

The obvious next step for the composers, and one which would be taken over and over again in the twentieth century, was to go on the offensive and organize their own ensembles and concerts. The ghettoization of contemporary music starts here.

Bartók with his first wife, Márta Ziegler, in 1912

The summer vacation of 1909 was spent, as usual, collecting folk material, and this time Bartók focused on the music of ethnic Romanians. A postcard to his old piano teacher dated 31 August gives an example of the vocal decorations he has been hearing, and he describes the songs as 'real coloratura arias'. On another postcard, sent on the same day to Etelka Freund, Bartók wrote down a violin dance tune ('Hora') in an unusual scale that he had never heard before. This scale stayed with him and eventually became the cornerstone of a method only slowly arrived at, and the recognizable basis of his most typical melodies and harmonies.

On 16 November Béla and Márta were married in a civil ceremony, in circumstances that have often been reported in the same, mysterious way. The story, apocryphal or not, and originally given out by Jenő Kerpely, the cellist of the recently-formed Waldbauer-Kerpely Quartet, is that Béla was giving Márta a piano lesson at home in the morning, and she stayed for lunch. In the afternoon the two went out, and returned to continue the lesson. When evening fell, Bartók announced to his mother that Márta would be staying for supper, as they were now married. The response of Mrs Bartók senior is not recorded.

4

Set design by Dezső Zádor
for the 1918 première of
Bluebeard's Castle at the
Budapest Opera House

Now hear the song.
You look at me, I look at you.
Our eyes' curtain – the eyelids – opens
Where is the stage, inside or out,
Ladies and Gentlemen?

From the prologue to *Bluebeard's Castle*,
by Béla Balázs

Seven Doors all Barred and Bolted 1909-18

For almost two years Bartók had been composing piece after piece in a rush of inspiration. The Rozsnyai publishing house, in the wake of their initial interest in Bartók as an editor of teaching editions of piano classics, was now committed to issuing his original piano work as soon as each new piece was ready. Another company with a younger, more dynamic staff, Rózsavölgyi, got in touch with Bartók and published the String Quartet (score and parts) in 1909. It is unlikely that there was much of a market for piano music like the Bagatelles – Bartók had lost his standing in Budapest with the

A bi-lingual advertisement for Bartók's works published by Rozsnyai

ROZSNYAI KÁROLY kiadása BUDAPEST Edition KARL ROZSNYAI

BARTÓK BÉLA

ugyanebben a kiadásban megjelent zeneművei:	Kompositionen in dieser Ausgabe:
14 zongoradarab, Op. 6 . . . . K 5.— n. Tartalom (Inhalt): I. Molto sostenuto. II. Allegro giocoso. III. Andante. IV. Grave. V. Vivo. VI. Lento. VII. Allegretto molto capriccioso. VIII. Andante sostenuto. IX. Allegretto grazioso. X. Allegro. XI. Allegretto molto rubato. XII. Rubato. XIII. (Elle est morte . . . .) Lento funèbre. XIV. Valse (Ma mie qui danse . . . .) Presto.	**14 Bagatellen f. das Pianoforte,** Op.6. M. 5.— n.
Tiz könnyű zongoradarab . . . . . K 4.— n. Tartalom: Ajánlás. I. Paraszti nóta. II. Lassú ver- gődés. III. Tót legények tánca. IV. Sostenuto. V. Este a székelyeknél. VI. „Gödöllei piactérre leesett a hó". VII. Hajnal. VIII. „Azt mondják, nem adnak". IX. Ujjgyakorlat. X. Medvetánc.	**10 leichte Klavierstücke** . . . . M. 4.— n. Inhalt: Widmung. I. Bauernlied. II. Qualvolles Ringen. III. Tanz der Slovaken. IV. Sostenuto. V. Abend am Lande. VI. Magyarisches Volkslied. VII. Aurora. VIII. Volkslied. IX. Fingerübung. X. Bärentanz.
GyermekekneK. Apró darabok kezdő zongorá- zóknak **(oktávfogás nélkül)** magyarországi gyer- mek- és népdalok felhasználásával. I. **Magyar népdalok** 1. füzet (Az I. évf. végén) K 2.— n. II. **Magyar népdalok** 2. füzet (II. évf.) . . K 2.— n. Mind a 2 füzet egy kötetben . . . . . . K 3.60 n. III. **Magyarorsz. tót népdalok** 1. füzet . . K 2.— n. IV. **Magyarorsz. tót népdalok** 2. füzet. . K 2.— n. A III—IV füzet egy kötetben . . . . . . K 3.60 n.	**Für Kinder.** Kleine Stücke ohne Oktavenspan- nung für Anfänger mit Benützung ungarländischer Kinder- und Volkslieder. Heft 1. **Ungar. Volksl.** Nô. 1—21. (I. Jahrg.) M. 2.— n. Heft 2. **Ungar. Volksl.** No.22—42. (II. Jahrg.) M. 2.— n. Beide Hefte in einem Bande . . . . . . M. 3.60 n. Heft 3. **Ungarl. slovak. Volkslied.** No.1—21 M. 2.— n. Heft 4. **Ungarl. slovak. Volkslied.** No.22—42 M. 2.— n. Heft 3—4 in einem Bande . . . . M. 3.60 n.
Két elégia, zongorára, Op. 8/b . . . . . K 3.— n.	**Zwei Elegien,** für Klavier, Op. 8/b . . M. 3.— n.
Vázlatok, zongorára, Op. 9 . . . . K 2.40 n.	**Esquisses,** für Klavier, Op. 9 . . . . . . M. 2.40 n.
Gyászinduló zongorára . . . . K 1.60 n.	**Marche funèbre** für Klavier . . . . . M. 1.60 n.
Két portrait, Op. 5. Zenekarra. Vezérkönyv . . . . K 5.— n. Zenekari szólamok . . . . K 10.— n. Külön vonósszólamok . . . . à K 1.— n.	**Zwei Porträts,** Op. 5, für Orchester. Partitur . . . . M. 5.— n. Sämtliche Stimmen . . . . M. 10.— n. Doublier-Stimmen . . . . à M. 1.— n.

mainstream music audience which treated both him and Kodály with indifference, if not open antagonism – but piano arrangements of folk material may have had a stronger appeal.

As well as the bald harmonizations of the short *For Children* pieces, most of the other collections contain atmospheric transcriptions of folk tunes, like 'Este a székelyeknél' ('Evening with the Székelys') in Ten Easy Pieces. Bartók also made elaborate transcriptions of what he had recorded in the field, reproducing all the vagaries and spontaneous ornamentation of a real performance, like the *Három Csíkmegyei Népdal* ('Three Folk-songs from Csík County'), published by Rozsnyai in 1909. A third way of treating folk material is shown in *Két Román Tánc* ('Two Romanian Dances'), where the content is obviously folk-derived, but the composer has got to grips with it and used it as the basis of an elaborate piece of composition.

There was some interest in what Bartók and Kodály were doing outside Hungary, but strangely, considering their similar situations, no contact with the Viennese avant-garde composers, led by their spokesman Schoenberg. The two men had certainly heard of Schoenberg in 1909, but it was only three years later that Bartók heard any of the Austrian composer's music.

Just before Christmas 1909 Béla and Márta travelled to Paris. Armed with some letters of introduction which he picked up from Busoni in Vienna *en route*, Bartók intended to make contact with a number of French composers. This was the period when he was perhaps at his most open to the influence of French music and culture, and Kodály would have had no difficulty in steering his friend in this direction. Yet he failed to make the right contacts on this trip; he was dissuaded from making contact with Debussy, who was at that time sketching the Edgar Allan Poe double-bill he was never to finish, *The Fall of the House of Usher* and *The Devil in the Belfry*, and whose off-handedness was legendary.

Bartók did not know anything by Ravel at this stage – the name was given to him while he was there, and back in Budapest in January Bartók wrote that he intended to get some of the French composer's latest piano music. Not surprisingly, he turned down an offer to meet the elderly and ultra-conservative Saint-Saëns (he had already encountered him in Oporto), and he felt horribly patronized in his meeting with the head of the Schola Cantorum, Vincent D'Indy. Just at the

Leó Weiner, Bartók's colleague at the Academy and fellow-composer. Portrait by Róbert Berény, 1911.

time when progressive composers were side-stepping, and soon rejecting, the need to establish a conventional sense of key, with all that implied in structural terms, he had to endure D'Indy's comment that he could sense no key or form in the third movement of the Orchestral Suite No. 2. Clearly for Bartók such a criticism was hopelessly old-fashioned – D'Indy was simply missing the point. But in a letter of Bartók's, a few weeks later, outlining a recital programme, he gives a key for each of the thirteen Bagatelles he is proposing to play, even to the outlandish extent of D sharp minor (No. 7) and A flat minor (No. 11). The first Bagatelle, written in two keys simultaneously, he defines as being in C major. A little touch of irony, perhaps? The piece does end on a C major third, and the mixed keys might just be Bartók's way of spelling the messy altered chord that repeatedly resolves on to this major third. It is the major/minor descriptions that are the most surprising. Did Bartók feel that his audience of the time could not approach his music without such guides?

Something was finally achieved on this Paris trip, however, and Bartók's piano music found a few sympathetic ears. The Swiss pianist Rudolf Ganz expressed an interest, and the Hungarian piano teacher Sándor Kovács, a Bartók enthusiast, immediately began to organize a 'Festival Hongrois' in Paris. This imposing title actually describes a Saturday afternoon concert in the Hôtel des Modes, on 12 March 1910, introduced by the librarian of the Paris Conservatoire, Henri Expert. Music by Bartók (including thirteen of the Bagatelles),

Kodály, Dohnányi, Mihalovich, Arpád Szendy and Leó Weiner was played – a strong representation from the Budapest Academy – and as well as press reviews, there was some attempt to cover the concert and the composers in a longer article in *Le Figaro*. It was in the context of this event that the description 'jeunes barbares' was put forward as a faintly admiring umbrella term for the Hungarians; Bartók may have been referring to this the following year when he wrote his piano piece *Allegro barbaro*.

Less than a week after the Paris event came the first of two concerts of chamber music in Budapest, given by the Waldbauer–Kerpely String Quartet, whose young players were all friends of Bartók and Kodály. Kodály was the focus of the first concert (17 March), and his String Quartet and Cello Sonata shared the programme with the Debussy and Ravel quartets. Bartók played the piano in this concert and in the following one two days later, devoted to his music alone. As well as his Quartet and Bagatelles, older works like the Piano Quintet were included.

The Waldbauer-Kerpely Quartet in March 1910, when Bartók's First String Quartet was first performed (left to right): Jenő Kerpely (cello), Bartók, Imre Waldbauer (first violin), Antal Molnár (viola), Kodály, János Temesváry (second violin)

If the concerts were meant as a musical contribution to the
Hungarian avant garde, then it is surprising that Bartók choose
to present the old as well as the new. Perhaps he simply wanted to
demonstrate his breadth of styles, or to show that the unfamiliar was
rooted in the familiar. Bartók's programmes in his various spells as
a performer often give the impression that he is demonstrating
something to his listeners; there is a sense that he does not want to
tax the audience too much, either with too much music, or with too
much of one style – even to the extent of hardly ever playing entire
pieces. But there is a paradox involved in this: while he instinctively
recognized the need to win an audience over, his platform behaviour
showed no great desire to please. It seems as if Bartók was well-
disposed towards his audience but unable to demonstrate it. It was not
simply that he did not cut a dashing figure on platform; his bows and
his acknowledgement of the audience's applause were awkward and
graceless, and even his absorption in the music was not picturesque.

After the concerts Bartók wrote to Kovács in Paris about how
successful Kodály's evening had been. Without a trace of self-pity he
records that his friend's music is seen as much more 'gentle and
humane' than his own. All the attention the concerts attracted must
have made the two composers feel that they had arrived. There was
interest not only from the Budapest publishers, but from a Parisian
company as well, and two pieces were accepted for a festival in Zurich
(Kodály's quartet and Bartók's Rhapsody). Still, this shows that it was
Bartók's earlier music that was making the best impression with the
general public.

Nyugat, not surprisingly, saw the concerts in epoch-making terms.
'The date of the two concerts … at which these two young men
appeared on the stage as comrades-in-arms, holding hands, should
be recorded for the future'. To the staff and supporters of *Nyugat*
Bartók was recognizably the more daring musician: the painter Róbert
Berény went so far as to claim that the String Quartet contained 'not
one single harmonic sequence which anyone has ever used before
him.' The phrase, of course, is nonsense, but it does give a flavour
of the partisanship of the time.

In May the Zurich concert went ahead, and Bartók's Rhapsody
was duly performed and applauded. When Bartók went to attend the
concert he met Frederick Delius, and the two men corresponded over
the following few months. The name of Percy Grainger soon cropped

Bartók with Béla Balázs, his librettist for *Bluebeard's Castle* and *The Wooden Prince*, setting out on a trip, 1917

up, and Bartók asked for some sort of introduction. Though Bartók would have been keen to contact a composer whose folk-song enthusiasms matched his own, the Australian's subjective approach, later to descend into dubious anthropology, could hardly have impressed him. But Bartók was obviously determined to find out as much as possible of every development in music, and this search for the new continued until the 1920s, when he finally won through to the creation of something that was unquestionably his own.

Folk-song collecting is discussed in the letters to Delius, and Bartók writes that he would like this to be his main occupation: 'teaching the piano to untalented youngsters who look upon music as a means of earning their living is truly not a thing I can feel any enthusiasm for.' But Bartók was at least as guilty as his pupils in relying on music as the means of earning his own living, and concern for his pension was one of the factors that kept him delaying his departure from Hungary at the end of the 1930s.

If there were any doubts that his enthusiasm for Strauss had dissipated, the review he wrote for the music journal *A Zene* ('Music')

in April 1910 of the first Budapest performance of *Elektra* makes it clear in one word: disappointment. The next orchestral work that Bartók finished (in August) showed that, at least in terms of orchestral colour, Debussy had firmly pushed Strauss aside. *Két kép* ('Two Pictures') are characteristically a coupling of slow and fast pieces, the fast one a rather casually composed sequence of dances in a regular rhythm, in anticipation of the *Dance Suite* of thirteen years later. The first movement 'Virágzás' ('In full flower') shows the strong influence of Debussy-ish elements in an approach to texture and colour that would be developed in his next major work. There are also some dramatic touches to the piece – emphatic phrases that seem to be saying something, and tolling bells through a gauze of blurring harps.

The announcement of an opera competition, named in honour of László Erkel, provided the impulse for Bartók to write his only operatic work, *A Kékszakállú herceg vára*, ('Duke Bluebeard's Castle'). His collaborator was the writer Béla Balázs, an old university friend of Kodály, whose family home in Szeged, on the Hungarian plain, had been the base for one of the first folk-song collecting trips. Balázs was born Herbert Bauer; the choice of a Hungarian *nom de plume* sprang from his desire to see a national literary culture come into being. Like all contributors to *Nyugat*, his sights were trained on Western Europe, and he had been Kodály's travelling companion when the composer went to Paris in 1907.

Earlier perhaps than either Bartók or Kodály, Balázs had come to understand the difficulties that his generation of artists faced. Their flagship may have been named after the West of their dreams, but disillusionment quickly set in with the decadent culture they encountered in the real west. On the other hand, for Hungarian artists to look at home for inspiration meant to seek out selectively a part of the native culture uncontaminated by petty nationalism. Balázs wanted to create 'a great Hungarian culture … a spiritual rebirth which would cleanse the present of its journalistic art and clownish science.' The musicians found their focus in the music of the peasants, of all the ethnic groups within the country's borders. Balázs achieved something similar in *Bluebeard's Castle*, where the native element is provided by the evocation of a ballad.

Balázs wrote his one-act 'mystery play' on Bluebeard between 1909 and 1910, with his direct source Maeterlinck's play *Ariane et Barbe-*

Bleue of 1902, set five years later as a three-act opera by Paul Dukas. The story of the multiple wife-killer was fixed by Perrault in his collection of tales of 1697, but has echoes throughout European folklore, not least in Hungary, where the ballad of Anna Molnár was a well-known variant. Maeterlinck astutely modernizes the story in making Ariane, Bluebeard's last wife, a positive character, unafraid of her husband, and unwilling to be dominated by him. When she discovers his previous wives in the castle dungeon, she berates them for being in thrall to darkness. In Balázs's play, Bluebeard's new wife is herself swallowed by the darkness.

Balázs was associated with the composer over a period of ten years, and left a number of impressions of the man which give some idea of how Bartók appeared to his contemporaries in his twenties and thirties. At first Balázs is caustic, writing in 1906 that Bartók is 'very modest, like a girl', but five years later, at the time of their collaboration, his tone has changed to religious awe: 'a most moving and most marvellous man. His frail, weak delicate body ... seemed as if it moved in robes in front of an altar.'

Balázs intended his one-act reworking of *Bluebeard* to be set to music by Kodály, but when in 1910 he gave a reading of the text, with Bartók and Kodály both present, it was Bartók whose imagination was fired by it. Of the three stage works Bartók composed music for, this is the one where he seems most directly involved in the dramatic content. There was surely a personal resonance for him in this story of a husband who is afraid to reveal himself, and a wife who wants to break down his defences. So it was Balázs's libretto he chose to set when he decided to enter the opera competition.

The opera opens with a spoken prologue of a minstrel introducing a ballad, asking his audience whether the events of 'once upon a time' which they are about to see occurred 'without or within'. This folksy quality continues in Balázs's use throughout of the traditional eight-syllable metre of old Hungarian ballads; the listener is lulled with its banal repetitions, 'Megyek, megyek, Kékszakállú' ('I'm coming, I'm coming, Bluebeard'), or 'Szépek, szépek, százszor szépek' ('beautiful, beautiful, a hundred times beautiful').

As the minstrel finishes speaking, the curtain rises on a great circular Gothic hall. We are in the land of decadent fables, beloved of *Nyugat*, and pictured by Károly Kós and Lajos Kozma. Bluebeard is

This 1954 set design for *The Wooden Prince* by Gustáv Oláh evokes the Symbolist Gothic style of the original (based on Vajdahunyad castle, see p. 23).

escorting his new wife Judith to his castle. She has left behind her
betrothed to follow him, and her family has sounded the alarm and
is setting off to find her. She is determined to remain with her husband, however: 'If you drive me away I'll wait at your door, lie down
on your threshold.' Judith follows Bluebeard into his dark castle, and
the door closes behind them. Once in the hall, where she puts out
a hand against damp walls, she comes across seven locked doors. She
demands to see what lies behind each door, and one by one Bluebeard
consigns the keys to her, reluctantly at first, then enthusiastically, and
finally with resigned pessimism. The opened doors reveal in succession Bluebeard's torture-chamber, his armoury, his treasury, his
garden, and his lands, and each new opened door lets in more light
to the castle. Everything that Judith discovers behind the doors is
marked with blood, and the sound which registers this, a stabbing
dissonance superimposed on the texture, reveals that the unseen
dampness on the castle walls was also blood.

The sixth door opens to shows a lake of tears, and the castle begins
to darken again. The last door provokes a battle of wills between husband and wife, but eventually Bluebeard gives way and Judith opens
it to find his three former wives, not dead, but 'collected', prized and
adored, emotionally divorced from their husband. He crowns Judith
the wife of midnight; she goes to join the other wives and the door
closes behind them, leaving Bluebeard alone in his dark castle hall.

The combination of the heavy symbols, the struggle between the
man and the woman, and the expectations of what will be revealed
behind each door make for a compelling piece of theatre, powerfully
drawn in Bartók's seductive music. A characteristic of opera in the
twentieth century, in reality from Verdi's *Falstaff* (1893) onwards, has
been the reintroduction of the forms of absolute music, driven by
the orchestra, and linked in some way to the dramatic shape; Berg's
Wozzeck and *Lulu* are the apotheosis of this approach; the sonata
movement in *Lulu*, for instance, which accompanies Lulu's finally
successful scheme to entice her protector away from his fiancée, is
a virtuoso display of matching form to dramatic content. In
Bluebeard's Castle Bartók is doing something much simpler, but the
musical need to impose an overall form on the work led him to
assemble his first arch construction. He chooses the strongest possible
opposition of keys, to contrast the murky opening, the 'once upon

a time' of the ballad, and the return to darkness at the close, with a midpoint of devastating light.

Whatever the audible influences, and Debussy is the most glaring when his 'sunken cathedral' is borrowed to ring out loudly when the fifth door opens, the work is in many ways the first piece of mature Bartók. It contains elements, in the way it sounds and the way it is constructed, that Bartók would return to as late as the Concerto for Orchestra more than thirty years later. The revelations behind each door are painted in extraordinary orchestral colours, and each image is initially established by insisting on a key and a timbre: a bright D major trumpet chord for the treasury, dull chromatic A minor flurries of celesta and harps, flute and clarinet, for the lake of tears.

Bartók considered the opera his first vocal piece, a description that gives an indication of how he felt about both his early Lieder and his folk-song settings. The composer who found *Elektra* disappointing was not going to be tempted into mimicking the sort of post-Wagnerian shrieking that Strauss was still employing. Instead Bartók draws on his folk experience and writes simple falling vocal lines with small intervals between the notes. The singers' lines are not decorated; the writing is predominantly syllabic. Debussy's vocal writing, both in his songs and in his opera *Pelléas et Mélisande* may have been an inspiration, and although Bartók is unlikely to have seen a performance of *Pelléas* when he wrote his own opera (it was not seen in Budapest until 1925), he certainly owned a copy of the score, along with the *Chansons de Bilitis*. But where Debussy is often overwhelmingly conversational and relaxed, Bartók rarely abandons the folk-declamatory manner. The rhythmic setting of the text, and the types of melodic phrases given to the voices are rooted in Hungarian folk song, as a comparison with the Twenty Hungarian Folk-songs will immediately reveal.

Bartók finished his setting in September 1911, and adding a dedication to Márta, entered his vocal score for the competition. Perhaps it looked to the jury as if there were nothing interesting to sing in this opera, and very little to watch in terms of stage action. Whatever their reasoning, the piece was turned down. The chairman was István Kerner, who had conducted the triumphant première of *Kossuth* years before, but Bartók was dismissive of his interest in investigating new music. A year later Bartók was once again working

on the score; Emma Kodály had written a German singing translation, presumably with the intention of trying to promote the opera abroad. Bartók's revisions are chiefly concerned with the climax of the piece – Bluebeard's three-part solo where he sings about his previous wives, and the conclusion. This was put into its final form only at the time of the first performance six years later, and it is here that the work really takes off as a piece of drama in music. Bartók continued to tinker with details of the score even later, making alterations to the vocal lines in the mid-1930s, chiefly to accommodate the requests of a leading signer of the title role, Mihály Székely (who made two recordings of the opera).

Instead of waiting to be embraced by the Budapest music world (for which they had little respect), Bartók and Kodály continued their self-help programme. The idea of seceding from the artistic establishment had already taken hold in the visual arts: three years earlier the artists known first as *Keresők* ('The Seekers') and then as *A Nyolcak* ('The Eight') had formed their breakaway group in opposition principally to the prevailing standards in Hungarian art, but by extension to the politics and social conventions of the time. Their closeness to the composers and performers of the new music is demonstrated by the fact that in May 1911 an exhibition by The Eight in the National Salon was the setting for a concert given by Bartók and the Waldbauer-Kerpely Quartet. Only in a culture where music was so important and widely practised, and so tied up with the national identity could it could be drawn into this radical movement, and it was not long before a New Hungarian Music Society (UMZE) was formed. A statement of intent and reforming plans for music education were published in *Zeneközlöny* ('Music Journal') to accompany the launch on 15 April 1911. Sándor Kovács appealed in print for subscribers to help with the setting up of an orchestra. As the relevant authorities had withheld a grant, the programme was reduced to a series of chamber concerts, beginning in November 1911.

The first of these featured Bartók playing music by Scarlatti, Couperin and Rameau. His thoughts on playing harpsichord music on the piano appeared in print in January, and their positive outlook gives an idea of what the performance was like: 'I think that any old clavecin music has to be performed in accordance with its character, utilizing all the perfections of the piano of today.' Also on the

Bartók and the Kodálys
in 1912, in the church at
Körösfő, the town where
Bartók's peasant furniture
was made

programme were several of Bartók and Kodály's 1906 folk-song arrangements, performed by an opera singer, Dezső Róna. The organizers were presenting some of the background to their musical outlook, the rediscovery of Baroque keyboard music and the revelation of folk-song. The context is still the conventional one of the chamber recital, and there is an element of compromise involved: harpsichord music played on a modern piano, and folk songs sung by an operatic voice. But in all, together with the Debussy and Ravel piano music which Bartók played at the second concert, these are the elements which Kodály saw as combining to effect his friend's 'liberation from the one-sided German orientation of his beginning'.

Schoenberg's music first came to Bartók's attention around this time. Of the Austrian composer's first so-called atonal works, it was the opus 11 piano pieces which he encountered when a pupil came to a lesson with a copy; he may also have known the Second String Quartet, with its vocal final movement, promising 'air from other planets'. In May 1912 Schoenberg wrote to Bartók to discuss various plans for performing pieces of new Hungarian music in Vienna. Schoenberg was planning a week of 'Unofficial Music in Austria', in response to the conservative repertoire of the 'official' Austrian Vienna Music Festival. The idea behind the undertaking is the same as that

of the UMZE, but ventures such as these had to wait until after World War I to take hold properly. Bartók corresponded only briefly with Schoenberg, mostly to plan reciprocal promotions of each other's music, but something of what he found in Schoenberg's music of this time took root as his own style developed.

After finishing *Bluebeard's Castle* in September, Bartók went on to write a short, concentrated piano piece, a controlled explosion of pounding energy which complements the elaborate and slow-moving opera. He uses the same opposition of dark and light areas, but here they are thrown together: bright outbursts of folk melody crash in on a background of dull, chugging chords. The piece was not accepted by Bartók's regular publishers, and was first published in an edition of *Nyugat* in January 1913, with the tempo indication, *Allegro barbaro*, as the title. There is one puzzling element in the varying number of bars given to the 'repeat till ready' chords which keep the pulse going: 8, 5, 3, 13. Such irregular phrase-lengths contribute to the savage, natural quality of the piece, but the numbers themselves were destined to become a controversial area in later analyses of Bartók's music.

Bartók's involvement with the UMZE dwindled after the first two concerts, and the undertaking itself fizzled out as a concert-promoting society in the first months of 1912. Rózsavölgyi now supplanted Rozsnyai in publishing Bartók's new work (Three Burlesques, written between 1908 and 1910, and the Four Dirges of 1910); but the rejection of his opera and the failure of UMZE prompted him to retreat from the city's musical life. In any case, in May 1911 the Bartóks had moved out from the city centre to what was then a village, Rákoszkeresztúr, but which has now been drawn into the leafy suburbs in the south-east of Pest. In the same month as the opera was finished Béla and Márta's only son, also named Béla, was born. Bartók's mother returned to Pozsony, and the young family set up home in a small house next door to the Vecseys. The following March they moved to a larger house in the same area, one with more peace and quiet for the composer (a recurring theme in the Bartók family's house-hunting) and they remained there until 1920.

The image we have of Bartók from this time is of a relaxed family man. Kodály and Emma Sándor had married in 1910, and the ties between the two couples were strong. There was much mutual involvement in each other's work: Márta regularly made neat copies

Bartók with his son Béla,
aged three, in the garden
of the Rákoskeresztúr
house, 1913

Bartók with Emma and
Zoltán Kodály. A pianist
and composer, Emma
Kodály first met Bartók in
1902 when, as Mrs Henrik
Gruber, she held open
house for young musicians.

of her husband's scores, while Emma, also a composer, and Béla helped each other in preparing anonymous copies of their works, when required to submit them in this way for composition competitions. The circumstances of the first revision of *Bluebeard's Castle* almost suggest an open discussion group: Emma's translation, written in ink in the score, has emendations in pencil by her husband, while it is highly likely that many of the musical revisions were prompted by suggestions from the Kodálys.

Nevertheless, contemporaries have remarked that the Bartóks' married life was not perfect. *Bluebeard's Castle*, of course, gives ample scope for speculation: was Stefi lurking behind the seventh door for him? In all his relationships with women, Bartók seems to have reverted to childish behaviour, and yet been attracted to the child-like woman. Márta seems to have continued to be the more mature partner in the relationship, and her devotion to Bartók is as much remarked on as her sunny, straightforward character. From Márta's description, his sense of humour was not very developed: 'He rarely laughed – mostly only when a letter arrived from abroad with an error in the address or he received first proofs of one of his works from one of his publishers abroad in which the Hungarian text was littered with misprints.'

Opposite, Bartók and
Kodály in the latter's
Budapest home

Bartók's intermittent vegetarianism probably began at this time: he continued to be attached to the benefits of Swiss health farms, and practised their various recommendations at home: sunbathing, exercises, and a ball-and-bat game. He did take up smoking during World War I, according to Márta to suppress hunger while food was in short supply, and continued to smoke for years. In 1917 Balázs was shocked to find that Bartók smoked and drank. It seems that Bartók was permanently concerned for his health and well-being: the small-pox incident in infancy and the subsequent concern on the part of his mother probably created the conditions for this. Balázs's description of the composer's frailness and young Béla's detailed report of the illnesses his father suffered suggest that he was right to be concerned. Nevertheless, as Bartók's son remarked, the physical demands of the folk-song collecting expeditions rarely seemed to have a negative effect on him. Bartók was still nominally Catholic, but when his son reached school age in 1917 he joined the Unitarian Church, to exempt the boy from Catholic religious instruction at school.

After moving to Rákoskeresztúr, Bartók's desire to compose left him again. He was still teaching at the Academy, but apart from the Four Pieces for orchestra written, but not orchestrated, in 1912, he stopped writing and was no longer involved in performing. Instead he focused on folk music, from an academic point of view, possibly once more influenced by Kodály. Bartók was not interested in simply soaking up an idiom to help with expanding his musical vocabulary; he was beginning to see the folk material as a cultural artefact, something that could help to identify paths of migration of peoples and give evidence of contact between various cultures. So he began to correspond with other people outside Hungary involved and interested in his topic. He wrote to Erich von Hornbostel, head of the phonographic archive in Berlin, and one of the pioneers of ethnomusicology. He also offered some of his Slovakian material to the publisher whose earlier books in a series of Slovakian songs had given Bartók some of the *For Children* tunes.

It was Bartók's normal practice on field trips to rely on an interested local person to help him find informants and provide background information. This was how he first met Ion Buşiţia, a secondary-school teacher in Belényes (Beiuş, Romania), when collected material in Bihar county in 1909. Buşiţia had a wide interest

in sporting and outdoor pursuits, as well as in the subjects he taught: music, geometry and drawing. He and Bartók quickly became friends. They corresponded regularly for years, Bartók writing in Romanian, and the Bartóks stayed with Buşiţia and his family several times before World War I.

The outbreak of war and its aftermath, when Romania was a victor and Hungary bitter and vanquished, did nothing to rock their friendship. With his first letter, in January 1912, Bartók sent a volume of poetry by Endre Ady – significantly a collection which urged Hungary's ethnic groups to unite (already together, the poet says, in misery). Bartók's letters to Buşiţia, published only in the 1950s after the Romanian's death, show that Bartók is ahead of his time, that he

Bartók transcribing field recordings made on wax cylinders

is becoming an ethnomusicologist more than a plain folklorist, and understanding that there is far more to recording folk material than merely taking down the notes and words of songs. He was aware that the entire social context of the music had to be recorded as well. It was, after all, the Ethnographic Division of the National Museum in Budapest which helped to finance Bartók and Kodály's various trips. The material was consigned to the Division, and papers were published in its journal, *Ethnographia*. The Romanian Academy in Bucharest contacted Bartók in December 1911 offering to publish his Romanian material, and this resulted in his first book, *Romanian Folk Songs from Bihar County*, which appeared two years later in two editions, French and Romanian.

The Bartóks travelled to Scandinavia in the summer of 1912; according to their son, this was a conventional holiday, not a folk-song field trip. In any case, Norway, for all its fiddle tradition, was a folk-music disappointment to Bartók. His most ambitious field trip came the following year, when he went to North Africa. The arrangements to obtain letters of introduction to Algerian authorities were helped along by Géza Zágon in Paris. Again the Ethnographic Division was providing some of the funds, and Bartók also offered to write an article for the Paris *Revue Musicale*. With a certain bravado the composer claimed that the heat would be no problem for him, but after little more than a week he retreated from Biskra, where he was collecting, to Algiers, and then to Switzerland. A picture post-card from Biskra to Zágon records some of Bartók's first impressions of the Kabyle Arab music he was hearing: the tuning of the wind instruments, the limited melodic range, but above all, the effect that varying accents in bars of equal length has in superimposing a second rhythmic pattern. Bartók was hearing in the field the effect that Stravinsky had been perfecting in his scores for Diaghilev's Ballets Russes, and which only a month before had reached its most aggres-sively bouncy in *The Rite of Spring*.

On Friday 27 December 1912 Budapest was given the opportu-nity to experience the innovative genius of the Ballets Russes for itself. Diaghilev's company, for four years the sensation of Paris, was on a tour that included Berlin and Vienna as well as the Hungarian capi-tal. *Petrushka* was already in the company's repertoire, but Diaghilev chose less recent pieces for the Budapest Royal Opera House: *The*

Firebird, Les Sylphides and *Carnaval.* Bartók was in the audience to
hear Monteux conduct and see Nijinsky dance (in *Les Sylphides*). One
bonus of the enthusiasm that the company fired in the Budapest
audience was that Bartók was almost immediately commissioned by
the Opera House to write a ballet score.

The first mention of this comes the following August, when Bartók
was back from North Africa and staying at his sister's house. He
wrote to Zágon that 'a sentence of death was passed on me officially
as a composer' (referring to the rejection of *Bluebeard's Castle* a year
before), and proclaimed that, with folk music his only interest, he
would now compose 'for my writing-desk only'. The same letter
mentions the Opera House's 'defiance of official opinion' in commis-
sioning a ballet score, but as it turned out, it was years before the
commission was fulfilled and the ballet performed. The Opera House
may have thought that they had a potential Stravinsky on hand, able
to write a Hungarian *Firebird.* What Bartók eventually composed
suggests that he may have had a similar idea.

Bartók went on an extended trip to France in the early summer
of 1914 and was in Paris, armed with his collection of Arab recordings,
in June when Gavrilo Princip, on behalf of the Serbian 'Black Hand'
Society, and, it was claimed, the Serbian government, assassinated the
heir to the Austro-Hungarian throne, Franz Ferdinand, and his wife
Countess Sophie Chotek. The events that led to World War I were set
in motion, and Bartók returned to Budapest with Mrs Kodály before
war was officially declared. The conservative government of the
Hungarian Prime Minister István Tisza had been considering a war
with Serbia for years, to be able to expand Hungarian territory in the
Balkans; the assassination gave them the ideal opportunity, but in
July they backed the Austrians in specifically denying any intention
of annexing Serbia if it were defeated. In Hungary, as in the other
European countries, the declaration of war in August was accompanied by a wave of nationalist enthusiasm; it increased in the follow-
ing year, when the country's old ally, Italy, joined the war against the
Austrians and Germans.

Bartók, in contrast, felt mentally paralysed by the outbreak of
war. Aged thirty-three he was turned down for military service in
November, because of being underweight, but he would not have
been fighting with any of the enthusiasm of his countrymen. His

first concern was with the plight of the peasants, whom he clearly valued over the middle and upper class of Hungary.

He continued to make some field trips during the first few years of the war, but these were gradually curtailed and eventually came to an end completely. It was as early as 1918 that Bartók and Kodály stopped collecting in Hungary, and the massive work of transcribing and classifying began to be tackled systematically. For Bartók, there was no question about the value of transcription, but ethnomusicologists since his time have regarded this sort of endeavour, writing down what has been recorded, as unnecessary. Whatever the source of the recorded examples, they have to be squeezed into the lines and spaces of European musical notation, and compromises will inevitably be made. Bartók faithfully notates every little decoration to the line the performer makes, and he is obliged to invent new symbols to express features that, although they may exist in various performance traditions of western music, are not notated.

Whatever creative block Bartók had been experiencing, depressed by the war, or by the way his career as a composer had once again stalled, events in 1915 started to release him from it. Until then he had apparently been talking about emigrating, and some of his colleagues recorded his mood as 'suicidal'. It was a trip to Slovakia which began to effect a change. That summer he, Márta and young Béla travelled to Zólyom County, and in September, possibly when his wife and son had returned to Budapest, he researched in the area of Kisgaram, in the same county. As always, he looked for a local person to help him as a guide to the area; here he was led to the chief forester, József Gombossy, and to his daughter Klára, a bright, energetic and precocious girl, who decided to help Bartók with his research. Klára, aged fifteen and still at high school, was having piano lessons from a local woman, a certain Mrs Gleiman. When Bartók first met the family, he asked Klára to play something, but she refused, saying that she preferred reading her books and walking in the forest. This can only have struck a chord with Bartók the nature-lover, and the two started to take long walks together, on which Klára talked about the poetry she wrote. Bartók was undoubtedly drawn to this girl and impressed by the poems which she gave him, yet it seems that he did not hesitate to show some of these to his wife when he returned to Budapest shortly afterwards, remarking on their precocity. In February 1916 he set three of her poems to music,

Bartók's photographs taken on field-trips. Two shepherds are shown; one plays the carved wooden long pipe (*hosszú furulya*), the other a bagpipe (*duda*).

in a style that matches their gushiness, almost to the point of
Expressionist parody. The first poem he set was 'Spring':

My love is not like the pale moon in the sky
which looks down on the water.
My love is the burning sunlight of midday,
full of strength and love.

On my lips is a burning kiss like the rose
in my eyes flaming trees burn
and in my body, eternally youthful, a heathen burns.
The ecstasy of love is in my blood.

This was followed by a 'Summer' and 'Autumn' in the same vein.
In August he set two more poems, to make a complete work, the
first Lieder collection he had written since his Lajos Pósa settings of
his student days. One of the texts ('Night of desire') was by Mrs
Gleimann's daughter, the other, 'Winter', was a version of an existing
poem by Klára.

At the same time Bartók was starting to write piano music again,
most of it simple, with a strong folk element. There were direct
transcriptions – the Romanian Folk Dances and Romanian Christmas
Songs – and a Sonatina where the folk material is used in classical
structure. February 1916 was a month of inspiration: this was when he
also wrote the Suite Op. 14 for piano, where the different strains in his
piano writing, the folk-quotation, the folk-inspired and the totally
original, merge to create an utterly unmistakable personal idiom. The
first three movements have, in turn, a jogging two-four beat, a
frenzied waltz, and even an appearance from the Arabs of Biskra.
After this the bleak yearning of the last movement comes as a shock,
and it is tempting to search for some reference to Bartók's feeling for
Klára here. This should have been the fifth movement – there
was originally another slow piece between the first and second movements of the final version – but it was not published.

The Gombossy songs were assembled as Op. 15, but for years the
author's name was not revealed. Only three of Bartók's songs were sent
to his post-war publisher, Universal Edition in Vienna, but they were
never published in his lifetime. The lack of an author's name meant

*Opposite, the art magazine
MA devoted a special issue
to Bartók in February 1917.
Reproduced on the cover is
the piano postlude to the
first Gombossy setting, Az
én szerelmem ('My love').*

IRODALMI ÉS KÉPZŐMŰVÉSZETI FOLYÓIRAT

Szerkesztőség és kiadóhivatal: Bpest, V. Visegrádi-u. 15.	Szerkesztik: KASSÁK LAJOS és UITZ BÉLA	Előfizetési ár Magyarországon: Egy évre 10 K, félévre 5 K.

TARTALOM: Bartók Béla: Kottarészlet. / **Kassák Lajos:** Napraköszöntés (vers Bartók Bélának). / **Náray Miklós:** Bartók Béla (tanulmány.) / **Barta Sándor:** Épülő ház (vers.) / **Berény Róbert:** Bartók Béla portréja (olajfestmény.) / **Bartók Béla:** Zongorakompozició (kottamelléklet.) / **Szélpál Árpád:** Tüntetés (vers.) / **Kádár Erzsébet:** Versek. / **Barta Sándor:** Tónus (vers.) / **Uitz Béla:** † Rodinról.

BARTÓK BÉLA : Kottarészlet

that the copyright could not be assigned. Bartók's continuing association with the avant garde in Hungary is shown by the appearance of his music in the periodical *MA* ('Today'), recently founded by Lajos Kassák, leader of the latest radical artistic movement, the Activists. *MA* was started in response to the government's ban on Kassák's anti-war arts journal *A Tett* ('The Deed'). The front cover of the issue of *MA* which appeared on 1 February 1917 had a facsimile of the piano coda to the first of the opus 15 songs, while inside was reproduced the entire last movement of the piano suite. Bartók immediately went on to write more songs, settings of Endre Ady this time; the result is a more mature and considered piece of work, but undoubtedly composed in response to the crisis that his feeling for Klára had prompted.

Bartók had met Ady, fleetingly, in November 1913, at the time of The Eight's third and last exhibition; he considered him 'the best poet of his generation' and perhaps felt the need to set some love poetry that allowed him to express, through another man's words, what he was currently experiencing. The style of the settings is similar to that of the Gombossy songs – a melodic recitation, with piano commentary. All this music, written at precisely the same time, has features in common (the first Ady song and the last movement of the Suite, for example), but the two sets of songs stand rather apart, both in terms of form and content, from the rest of Bartók's work. When they were published in 1920, Bartók dedicated the Ady songs ('with true friendship and love') to a member of the *Nyugat* circle, Béla Reinitz, an amateur songwriter and music critic who had long championed Bartók's work. There is some evidence that Reinitz's simple song-settings of Ady poems may have been a model for Bartók's vocal style in his own settings.

In April 1916 Bartók was once again in Slovakia, staying at the castle of a family in Nyitra county. Armed with a ballet libretto, again by Balázs, he was finally working to fulfil the opera house commission, and composing *A fából faragott királyfi* ('The Wooden Prince', or more accurately, 'The Prince of Carved Wood'). The libretto had first appeared in *Nyugat* in 1912, and it had always seemed to Bartók a potentially perfect companion piece in a double-bill with *Bluebeard's Castle*. That this eventually became the case goes only some way to excusing Bartók's apparent unawareness of how expensive and impractical a project this could be.

Once again Balázs's mixture of the fantastic and symbolic has a message about relations between men and women. Two little castles lie on either side of a stream. In one lives a prince, in the other a princess. A fairy who lives in the forest discourages the princess from meeting the prince, and when the prince in turn tries to cross the bridge to the other castle, the fairy puts a spell on the stream to prevent him from crossing. Unable to attract the princess's attention from the other side of the stream, the prince eventually makes a wooden puppet and dresses it with his own hair, which he has cut off, and with his own cloak. He entices the princess with this, and she, not interested in the real prince, dances with the puppet. It is only when she tires of the wooden version of the prince that she tries to seduce the real one, who has had his hair and cloak restored to him by the fairy. He ignores her, and in frustration she cuts off her own hair and throws off her cloak. At this he approaches her and eventually succeeds in comforting the princess.

Bartók, c. 1916, the period of his liaison with Klára Gombossy

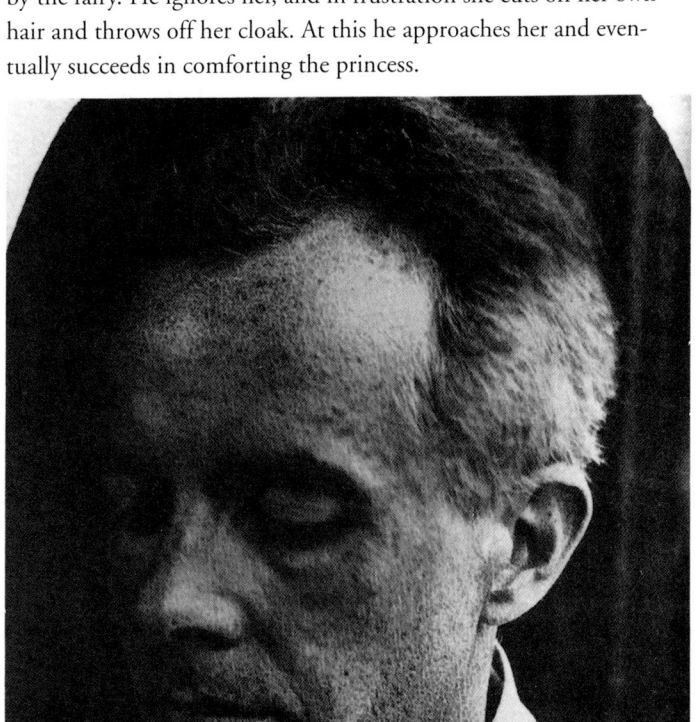

Photographs of Bartók at this time show him apparently in a dreamy mood, divorced from the catastrophic events all around. Is he playing the romantic lover? He certainly seems to have identified himself and Klára with the prince and princess of the ballet. This interlude ended in September 1916, and perhaps it was the intrusion of outside events that helped to waken him. At the end of August that year, Bartók was in Slovakia while his wife and son were far away in Transylvania. Romania entered the war on the side of the Entente on the 27th, and it was only a matter of time before they invaded Transylvania. When this duly happened Márta made a hasty retreat with young Béla and went directly to confront Bartók; the result was that his relationship with Klára came to a definite end, and husband and wife were reunited.

In the war years Bartók was clearly working without any overt nationalism, in contrast to almost every other European composer: we think of Debussy signing his sonatas 'musicien français'. For this

The Royal Opera House in Budapest, designed by Miklós Ybl, was one of the most sumptuous and technically modern in Europe when it was inaugurated in September 1884. Both *The Wooden Prince* and *Bluebeard's Castle* were premièred here.

Design by Gusztáv Oláh for
a tree costume in a 1952
Budapest production of *The
Wooden Prince*

reason alone, *The Wooden Prince* seems like a work set apart from its
time; the Ravelian opening alone suggests the opulence of a disappearing world. At the end of 1916 arrangements were already under
way to have the work performed the following year, and the première,
in the Royal Opera House in Budapest on 12 May 1917, was Bartók's
first popular success.

The ballet was seen in a triple-bill, sandwiched between a Gluck
opera, *Le Cadi dupé*, and a comic ballet on music by Mozart. Much
of what has been written about *The Wooden Prince* has been concerned
solely with Bartók's music, but some of the credit for the success of
the première must go to the choreographer and the dancers. Again
Balázs's colourful recollections in his diary give a strong flavour of the
event: the hard work of the conductor Egisto Tango, the huge number of rehearsals, the bafflement of the original choreographer, and
especially the attitude of the music critics, whose ready-written

Kezdete 6 órakor.

Magy. Kir. Operaház.

Szombaton, 1917. május hó 12-én

(bérletszünet 122 szám, részben felemelt helyárak)

I.

uj betanulással:

A RÁSZEDETT KÁDI

Vig dalmű egy felvonásban. Szövegét irta Krastl Frigyes, forditotta Ábrányi Emil. Zenéjét szerzette Gluck Kristóf.
Az előadást vezényli Kerner István, rendezi Bródy István.

A kádi ...	... Venczell Béla	Omar, varga ... ... Dalnoki Viktor dr.
Fatime, a felesége	... Maleczky Bianka	Omega, leánya ... ... Bársony Dóra
Zelmira ...	... Hajdu Ilona	Aga ... ... Kertész Ödön
Nuradin	... Szügyi Kálmán	Történik a kádi házában.

15 perc szünet.

II.

először:

A FÁBÓL FARAGOTT KIRÁLYFI

Táncjáték egy felvonásban. Szövegét irta Balázs Béla, zenéjét irta Bartók Béla. — Rendezte Balázs Béla.
Koreografiáját készitette Zöbisch Ottó. Az előadást vezényli Tango Egisto.

Táncolnak:

A királyfi	... Pallay Anna	Az erdő
A királykisasszony ...	... Nirschy Emilia	A patak
A tündér	... Harmat Boriska	A három virág } a teljes tánckar
A fabáb	... Brada Ede	

15 perc szünet.

III.

ÁMOR JÁTÉKAI

Vig ballet egy felvonásban, irta Mozart. Szinpadra alkalmazta Hevesi Sándor. Vezényli Rékai Nándor. Rendezi Zöbisch Ottó.

Ámor ... ... Keresztes Mariska	Táncosnő ... ... Pótz M.	Kapitány ... ... Toronyi Gyula
Colin-Maillard ... Kiss Janka	Arlechino ... Keszthelyi J.	Kinai iány ... Komlós Margit
Colombina ... Fellegi Laura	Clorinda ... Kranner Ilona	Kinai ember ... Ádám Győző
Táncos ... ... Brada Ede	Pantalone ... Smeraldi Cézár	

Kezdete 6 órakor, vége 9½ óra után.

MŰSOR:

Vasárnap, május 13-án; **Tosca** (Anthes György felléptével) ... ... Kezdete 6½ ó.
Kedden,   „   15-én : **A fából faragott királyfi** (másodszor). **A rászedett kádi.**
Ámor játékai. (Rendes helyárak) ... ... Kezdete 6 ó.

HELYÁRAK:

HELYEK	Május 12-ére napi ár	Május 12-ére elöv. ár	Rendes napi ár	Rendes elöv.ár	HELYEK	Május 12-ére napi ár	Május 12-ére elöv. ár	Rendes napi ár	Rendes elöv.ár
	K f.	K f.	K f.	K f.		K f.	K f.	K f.	K f.
Páholy: földszinti ...	47 —	49 —	37 —	39 —	Támlásszék a XVIII—XXIII. sorban	7 20	8 20	4 20	5 20
„ I. emeleti ...	47 —	49 —	37 —	39 —	II. em. páholyülés az I. sorban	8 20	9 20	5 20	6 20
„ II. „ II. szám .	47 —	49 —	37 —	39 —	„ a II.	6 20	7 20	4 20	5 20
„ II. „ 2—5. .	25 —	27 —	19 —	21 —	III. em. erkélyszék az I.	6 10	6 60	4 10	4 60
Zsöllye ...	16 20	17 20	10 20	11 20	„ a II—V. sorban	5 10	5 60	3 10	3 60
Támlásszék az I—II. sorban .	13 20	14 20	8 20	9 20	„ a VI—IX.	4 10	4 60	2 60	3 10
„ a III—VI. ,	12 20	13 20	7 20	8 20	III. em. zártszék az I. sorban	4 10	4 40	2 60	2 90
„ a VII—IX. ,	10 20	11 20	6 20	7 20	„ a II.	3 10	3 40	2 10	2 40
„ a X—XIII. ,	9 20	10 20	5 20	6 20	„ a III—IV. sorban	2 10	2 40	1 60	1 90
„ a XIV—XVII. sorban .	9 20	9 20	4 70	5 70					

Jegyek válthatók: a napi és a vasárnapi előadásokra a Hajós-utcai pénztárnál, a műsoron hirdetett más előadásokra a Dalszinház-utcai pénztárnál naponként délelőtt 9—1-ig és délután 3—5 óráig (Telefon: 22—49.); ezenkivül egész napon át a következő elárusitó helyeken: 1. Bárd Ferenc és Testvére zeneműkereskedése: Kossuth Lajos-utca 4. szám (Standard palota. Telefon 6—56. és 57—28.) és Andrássy-ut 1. szám. (Telefon 25—13. és 57—08. szám.) 2. Rózsavölgyi és Társa zeneműkereskedése : Szervita-tér 5. (Telefon 10—08.) és Andrássyut 45. (Telefon 148—82.)

Esti pénztárnyitás a szinházban 5½ órakor.

Left, playbill for the
première of *The Wooden
Prince* at the Budapest
Opera House, May 1917

reviews were made redundant by the wave of enthusiasm which
swept from the gallery downwards at the end of the performance. The
optimistic idea underpinning all this is that despite the entrenched
conservatism of the professionals and the audience in the stalls, the
voice of the people spoke out in favour of the 'revolutionaries' who
had created the work, and the strength of their enthusiasm overwhelmed the opposition. Balázs wrote:

> *It was a success the like of which was never recalled at the Opera. They
> called me back at least thirty times. They raved for more than half an
> hour. The next day the papers gave Bartók full recognition, but me mostly
> abuse ... [It] might have pleased me if they had acknowledged one thing
> ... the fearful work I did for Bartók, and that I did it for him alone.
> That I broke his symphonic music down for the stage, since it is devoid of
> all stage timing and spacing ... that I drilled music which musicians do
> not understand into houseporters' daughters, that I got it across that every
> movement corresponded to a phrase of the music (with ballerinas who
> were not even accustomed to doing this to the music of Delibes).*

Not surprisingly, this was the last time Bartók and Balázs
collaborated.

Musically *The Wooden Prince* can be an unsatisfactory work,
certainly when performed as a concert piece, and Bartók often gives
the impression of not being totally at ease. The score is made up of
seven dances, framed by a Prelude and a Postlude. The titles of the
dances indicate how schematic the libretto is: Dance of the Princess
in the Forest, Dance of the Trees, Dance of the Waves, etc. There are
some inspired musical moments – the Prelude is like the music for
the dawn of the folk-world – and brilliant orchestral touches, like the
saxophone waltz for the Dance of the Waves. There is greater sense
of breadth than in *Bluebeard's Castle*, but less tension. Bartók made
a suite from the ballet in 1931, and this was also premièred at the
Opera House, conducted by Dohnányi.

Bartók's Second String Quartet, written during the same period,
stands in strong contrast to the ballet score. Where *The Wooden Prince*
is prolix, the Quartet is taut, and where the ballet often has derivative
flashes, the Quartet is concentrated, mature Bartók. The touches of
Debussy and Ravel, and even a suggestion of his old Straussian sound

in *The Wooden Prince* indicate some lack of confidence in a musical idiom based on folk material, but the Quartet finally and fully justifies Bartók's method. The question of harmony is dealt with in a way which draws both melodic lines and the harmonic context from the same motifs, and the polyphonic texture of the first movement creates the conditions for Bartók to pursue this linear approach in the most fluid, technically brilliant single movement he had yet written. The energetic Scherzo is a *tour de force* of unstoppable rhythmic vitality as well as string sonority: ringing plucked octaves, clattering unisons and screeching dissonances. And an effect that will return repeatedly, material which is first heard in duple time comes back in breakneck triple time. In common with Bartók's other works of the time, there is an enigmatic last movement; more than simply a slow movement, it is an expression of a bleakness that cannot be consoled.

5

'Lajos Kossuth's message:
Long live the Republic'. In
Jenő Paizs Goebel's 1918
poster a red-capped
Hungarian soldier throttles
the Habsburg eagle. The
independence from Austria
for which Kossuth fought
has become a reality.

*It was as if a plague of locusts had devastated
the place. Consumed and exhausted, the town
lay on the rubbish heap. The expensive
porcelain shelves in the window of the baroque
Konditorei displayed a single, desolate scone.
Trams which had been painted under
Communist rule were still to be seen in their
revolutionary scarlet with revolutionary slogans
daubed across them, dashing suicidally through
town like refugees from a mental asylum. But
there were also encouraging signs of improve-
ment. Middle-class passengers on the tram were
no longer afraid to stand up to the bullying
conductress who addressed them rudely ... Men
once again began to give up their seats to ladies.
It was a new and glorious flowering of the age
of chivalry.*

From *Anna Édes*, by Dezső Kosztolányi

A Strain of Harsh Asceticism 1918–30

Any illusions the Hungarian people may have had about military glory and honour had disappeared after three years of devastating modern warfare, which left every second man in the army a casualty. By 1917 Hungarian soldiers were deserting in droves, industrial workers were repeatedly on strike, and the cities were desperately short of food. It was as if the people of Hungary had sniffed the air and sensed the disaster and humiliations to come. But their disaffected agitation could not affect the still-unresolved direction of the war: although the great stalemate of the Western Front had still not broken by the beginning of 1918, the central powers were to launch an offensive that spring which might have brought them victory. There were advances on the Eastern Front too, during February and March, when the German army closed in on Petrograd, and dealt with the Bolshevik administration.

In January 1918 the Austro-Hungarian military involved Bartók in a concert of soldiers' folk-songs, given in Vienna. The Queen of Hungary, consort of the new Emperor-King Karl, attended along with what Bartók described to Buşiţia as 'a galaxy of *Gott erhalte* backers, gem and decoration wearers and musical ignoramuses'. In less than a year the Habsburg empire would be gone, and the glittering audience consigned to the past as Hungary was overwhelmed by waves of revolution.

The concert included arrangements by Bartók of soldiers' folk-songs from two of the three main ethnic traditions within Hungary – Magyar and Slovakian. Romanian songs were originally programmed, but to keep the concert from overrunning, and because of Romania's enemy status, these were ultimately left out. As well as choral arrangements, sung by the Viennese Männergesangverein, solo songs were on the programme, accompanied by Bartók at the piano. In wartime, all sorts of alterations were made to the material, for political reasons; texts were edited and Slovakian songs were sung in German, but it must have been a source of pride for Bartók to hear the fruits of more than ten years of research presented in an establishment setting.

Bartók in 1923, the year of
his *Dance Suite*

The concert gave rise to further developments: the prestigious
music publisher Universal Edition, founded in 1901, and a specialist
in contemporary music, immediately contacted the composer. An
agreement to publish his music was worked out over the next months
and finalized in June. Among the first works to be published was the
Five Slovak Folk-songs for men's chorus which had been heard at the
Vienna concert. UE was to publish all Bartók's works until the end
of the 1930s, and they took on not only the new pieces, but also the
music Bartók had been writing during the war, the Suite Op. 14,
the Sonatina and *The Wooden Prince*.

Bartók's programme note, in German, on the melodies of the
Hungarian soldiers' songs shows him establishing for the first time
in print the terminology and theory of Hungarian folk music which
both he and Kodály were to develop in their later writings. The open-

ing paragraph throws up the casual interchange of 'folk' and 'peasant' music that is frequently found in his writings. Here, of course, he is using German terms, and 'Volk' has a larger meaning than Bartók would have intended, but for years, writing in Hungarian, he would continue vaguely to equate 'folk' (nép) with 'peasant' (paraszt).

Bartók identifies two strains, old and new, in Hungarian folk music. Old melodies are characteristically in one of the old Church modes of Gregorian plainchant, although Bartók identifies an even older strain (among the Transylvanian Székely people) of pentatonic (five-note) tunes. The four lines of the song are set to four different melodic phrases, and although the songs may be clearly in lines of six, eight or twelve syllables, the rhythm is fairly free; what Bartók, borrowing the terminology of Western music, classifies as *Parlando rubato* (freely reciting). Newer songs, which he considers to date from the last quarter of the nineteenth century, are mostly in the Church mode closest to a minor scale, or else unequivocally in a modern major scale. Phrases are repeated within the melody, and the rhythm is regular: what he and Kodály formerly described as a dance-step (*Tánclépés*) is now classified as *Tempo giusto* (strict time). The evolutionary theory is clear: first there were five notes, then seven of a mode, and lastly the seven of the modern European major scale. Originally singers recited their way through melodies, pausing and delaying as expression required; later they sang in strict dance rhythm.

The following month Bartók's arrangement for small orchestra of his six Romanian Folk Dances was performed in Budapest, and in March his Second String Quartet was given its first performance, by the Waldbauer-Kerpely quartet. The climax to this run of first performances came on Friday 27 May, when *Bluebeard's Castle* was finally produced at the Opera House in a double-bill with a revival of *The Wooden Prince*. For this performance Bartók made his last revisions to the conclusion of the opera, the resolution of Judith's final struggle with Bluebeard. Once again the conductor was Egisto Tango, for whom Bartók had nothing but admiration. He was pleased and flattered that Tango approached his work so conscientiously, preparing scores weeks before the beginning of rehearsals. Bartók compared him with Kerner, who did not open new scores until the day of the first rehearsal.

Kodály reviewed the event enthusiastically in his role as music critic for *Nyugat*, while opinions, as expressed in Budapest's daily press

were mixed. Some critics were more favourable than others, particularly those writing in the city's two German-language newspapers, but generally Bartók felt that *Bluebeard's Castle* got a better reception than the ballet. Balázs seems again to have borne the brunt of most of the negative criticism, and there was a definite rift between the two men from this time. Bartók does not seem to have spoken up for his librettist, and Balázs was certainly jealous of the way Bartók was embraced by the critics. When the right wing triumphed in Hungary at the end of the following year, Balázs went into exile; his works were proscribed in his native country, and consequently the opera and ballet he and Bartók had collaborated on remained unseen for years. Balázs was also bitter that he was being judged on work that was several years old, and that other names were now floated as possible collaborators for Bartók. Sándor Bródy, a short-story writer and playwright, was to have supplied a text for a projected opera; when it did not arrive on time Bartók went on to work with another dramatist, Menyhért Lengyel, at the time famous throughout Europe for his play *Tájfun* ('Typhoon'). Like other Hungarian playwrights of his generation, Lengyel later left the country and eventually worked in Hollywood as a screenwriter.

It seems that Bartók's old piano teacher, István Thomán was responsible for making the contact between the composer and Lengyel, whose scenario for *The Miraculous Mandarin*, the piece Bartók started to work on, had appeared in the *Nyugat* issue of New Year's Day, 1918. Balázs suspected that he was being marginalized because of the press response to his libretto, but in fact Bartók and Lengyel were already arranging to collaborate before *Bluebeard's Castle* reached the stage.

As a result of the successful coupling of *Bluebeard* and *The Wooden Prince*, Bartók could easily consider himself as the leading music representative of the Hungarian avant-garde movement. But the coupling did not survive for long. The following night the Opera House proceeded to mount the second performance of *Bluebeard* paired with a Saturday-night crowd-pleaser: Leoncavallo's *Pagliacci*. Was this in recognition of Bartók's success in a bastion of the establishment, or a sly attempt to deflate some triumphalism?

In the last summer of the war, Bartók went, as always, to his sister's home in Vésztő, before setting out for Transylvania with Tango, by

now a good friend with whom he was eager to share his enthusiasm
for peasant life and music. In August he went back to Nyitra county
in Slovakia, staying at the home of an aristocratic patron of the arts,
Baron Kohner. These two field trips were the last he ever made
in Hungary, and the destinations would soon be no longer part of
the country.

In September Bartók was back in Rákoskeresztúr, while Márta
continued her holiday in Vésztő; in a letter to her Bartók mentions
Lengyel's libretto, which he was now starting to set, writing as always
in short score, for piano, but on 8 October he fell ill with the Spanish
flu which was sweeping Europe, and which would eventually account
for more deaths than the war. By the time Bartók was well enough to
leave his bed at the end of the month, Hungary was in ferment, and
there was revolution on the streets of Budapest.

When the front line gave way in October, it was clear to Austria
and Hungary that defeat was inevitable. The Germans were already

negotiating peace with the Entente, and the Austrian Emperor responded to the American President Woodrow Wilson's Fourteen Points (under which the nations which wanted to break free from the Empire were guaranteed independence) by proposing a federal state. The Hungarian parliament declared itself independent and refused to allow autonomy for the country's various regions. On the 25th Count Mihály Károlyi formed a National Council, in opposition to the government, with liberal political reform its goal. Six days later, with the backing of the Territorial Army, Károlyi's forces gained control of Budapest in a bloodless coup, the so-called Chrysanthemum Revolution, named after the buttonholes which the victors and their supporters wore. At Padua on 3 November the Entente signed a separate peace agreement with Austria and Hungary, the King declaring that he would no longer take part in government. The republic of Austria was declared on 11 November, and Karl abdicated the next day. Five days later Hungary was also declared a republic.

The country of Hungary was shrinking by the day as areas seceded and neighbouring countries broke off the chunks they laid claim to. Croatia was the first to go, and the Czechs, Slovaks and others took advantage of the country's defeat. The Romanians moved into large areas of former Hungary, and annexed Transylvania in January 1919.

In the face of this, and the continuing chaos and famine, the well-meaning liberal democracy of Károlyi was able to last only until the following March. Károlyi was even photographed making his own selfless contribution to land reform by redistributing his own estate. But after a new, humiliating territorial demand came from the victorious allies, he resigned, and the very same day, 21 March, the Hungarian Republic of Councils was declared, with the governing council headed by the Communist leader Béla Kun. From the evidence of what was happening in nearby Vienna and Munich, it seemed to the Hungarian Communists that the revolution started in Russia was inevitably sweeping west. Allied to Soviet Russia, the Hungarian Communists proceeded to throw together Socialist institutions and a programme of social engineering while optimistically attempting to negotiate a settlement with the victorious powers of the Entente.

Bartók was suddenly thrust into the political limelight when the Communists appointed him a member of the Directorate of Music,

Following page, poster by Róbert Berény, 'To arms! To arms!' (1919). Berény took part in the Republic of Councils between March and August 1919, when this poster was created. After the revolution collapsed he moved to Berlin, but returned to Hungary in 1926.

along with Kodály, Dohnányi and Reinitz. He was even considered, for a while, as a possible director of the Opera House. This public role was in stark contrast to his desire, expressed at the beginning of the year, to be transferred from teaching to working in a newly-created museum department of folk music. Perhaps his retreat from public life in the preceding years had been misread as simple opposition to the ruling establishment, and it was thought that the radical quality of his music would be translated into administrative decisions. It is hard to imagine a man less likely to flourish in a political environment than Bartók; no one ever commented on his tactfulness, and his behaviour in public was never geared to easy social intercourse.

Under the Károlyi regime, the Academy of Music had seen its older staff pensioned off and replaced by younger men: Kodály and Dohnányi were put in charge, and started to reform the way the Academy was run. However, according to Bartók's later report on the changing events, the Republic of Councils was far less enlightened: it was their aim to impose ideology on every aspect of musical life. The 'Internationale' ('utterly devoid of both harmony and thought', in Bartók's words) was sung before every performance at the Opera, bureaucracy mushroomed, and the separate unions of musicians and craftsmen were merged.

Worst of all for the people of Budapest was the continuing famine. The Council's currency, which everyone was paid in, was not accepted either in the shops, or by peasants who could supply food. Bartering was the only solution, and Márta wrote to her mother-in-law with some details what could be achieved in this way: 'I get things from the peasant (pardon! our comrade field-labourer): with clothing. Thus I bought 60 eggs for a shirt, 30 litres of milk for a pair of stockings; of course I take it in instalments.'

The Soviet experiment was in a fragile condition throughout its entire existence, under threat both from outside (the Romanian army invaded Hungary proper in April to make sure they held on to Transylvania), and from within, by internal divisions. The country itself was split, with a rival, counter-revolutionary government based in Szeged in the south, an area occupied by the French. One of the members of this government was the Rear-Admiral Count Miklós Horthy, who was soon to take over command of the 'National Army' of opponents to the governing council. An uprising which started in

Gyula Derkovits's woodcut of 1928 is one of a series commemorating the 1514 Hungarian peasant uprising and its aftermath with obvious parallels with the White Terror of 1920.

Szeged in June quickly reached Budapest, only to be crushed by the council. In the east, the Romanians had crossed the River Tisza and were marching on the capital; but in the end it was the city's central workers' council which forced the removal of Kun and his government on 1 August. The leaders left for political asylum in Austria, and after a few days of an interim government, István Friedrich, a factory owner, seized power and the Romanian Army entered Budapest. The 'White terror' of rooting out communists and those imagined to be enemies, and their summary hanging, moved up from the country to grip the capital.

During all this upheaval Bartók had actually managed to finish the piano score of his pantomime, but in the circumstances, with death

and destruction all around, it is only fitting that the scenario he had on his desk was a macabre, ironic commentary on the Wagnerian ideas of love and self-sacrifice. In July he played his score through on the piano in István Thomán's house, with Márta, Thomán and Lengyel as his audience.

The Miraculous Mandarin was not orchestrated until the second half of 1924, when the Opera House in Budapest contacted Bartók about the possibility of its being performed, although in the event no production went ahead. By this time Bartók had written and scored his first popular orchestral work, the *Dance Suite,* and that experience no doubt informed the way he approached the orchestration of the pantomime: the vividness of the colours in the score is matched to the terse and direct descriptive quality of the music. The rigidity of *Bluebeard* and the relaxed breadth of *The Wooden Prince* have both disappeared and the result is one of Bartók's most arresting scores.

The piece finally reached the stage in 1926, in Cologne (in a double-bill with *Bluebeard's Castle,* sung in German), and in the face of a huge outcry it was instantly banned. Budapest had to wait until December 1945 for a performance, and even then there were alterations to the dramatic content. In both cases Lengyel's subject-matter, fairly typical of the decadent strain in *Nyugat* writing, was a stumbling-block for the guardians of morality, who reacted strongly against it.

The setting is a squalid, upper-storey room in a modern city, the den of three thugs. The noise and energy of the street outside penetrate the room. The thugs coerce their girl friend to stand at the window and entice men upstairs, so that they can rob them. The first to succumb is an old gallant; when he approaches the girl she insists on seeing his money, but he has none, and the thugs spring from their hiding-place and throw him out. The second client is a young student, whose tenderness touches the girl, but he has no money either, and is also thrown downstairs.

The girl returns to the window and ensnares her third customer. He is Chinese, portrayed as the sinister stereotype of the day: a threatening Mandarin with unblinking, hypnotic eyes. The girl dances for him, but he is unmoved. So she lands in his lap, and he suddenly begins to shake 'in feverish excitement', as the stage directions have it. He leaps up and chases her, but the three thugs spring out, and holding him down, take everything valuable he has. At the

Admiral Miklós Horthy,
leader of the counter-
revolutionary National
Army, crosses Liberty
Bridge into Pest in triumph,
November 1919

same instant they decide he has to die, and they smother him. But the Mandarin is not dead; he gets up and continues to chase the girl. The thugs are horrified, but they control themselves and stab him. Still he will not die, so they grab him and hang him from the light cord. To the eeriest sounds ever created by Bartók, the Mandarin's hanging body begins to glow in the dark. The girl now knows what will satisfy him. She orders the men to cut the Mandarin down, and she kisses him. Now his wounds begin to bleed and at last he dies.

Bartók catches every detail of this scenario with an almost photographic accuracy, from the ceaseless activity of the city street through the various eruptions of violence, right to the grim denouement. There is no doubt that Stravinsky's *Rite of Spring* has made its mark on the composer; Bartók was unselfish enough to have carried the score of the Stravinsky ballet around with him during rehearsals of *Bluebeard* in the hope that a performance could be mounted in the Opera House. But where Stravinsky is concerned with an outburst of energy and eventual catharsis of unnamed 'primitives' performing a ritual in a prehistoric setting, Bartók is writing music for real contemporary characters, melodramatic ones, perhaps, but familiar enough from popular film culture.

The upheaval of the latter half of 1919 touched Bartók directly when soldiers from the occupying Romanian army took over his house on the outskirts of Budapest. His request for a leave of absence from the Academy was passed on through Kodály, then deputy director, to the Minister of Culture, but within a month Bartók, Kodály, and Dohnányi had all been suspended. Tango lost his post at the Opera House in the same backlash, and at this point Bartók began to talk of emigrating. The violin professor Jenő Hubay, the favoured candidate of the right, was appointed director of the Academy in November 1919, and all the reforms of the preceding year were overturned.

This reflected in microcosm what was happening in the political life of the country as a whole. Horthy's National Army was growing, and taking over the parts of Hungary not occupied by the Romanians. By agreeing to the condition (put forward by the Entente) that democratic elections would be held, Hungary succeeded in having the Romanian army withdraw. Horthy entered Budapest in November, at the head of what was now a large force. The struggle between those

who wanted the king (who had abdicated from the Austrian throne but not the Hungarian) to return and those who felt he personally was unfit was solved by the election of Horthy as Regent, in a revival of a medieval institution with a precedent as recent as 1849.

The Treaty of Trianon in June 1920 established a new kingdom of Hungary that was around a third of its former size, with a third of its former population. In terms of territory, it lost out to the newly-formed Yugoslavia, Romania and Czechoslovakia (who together formed a little Entente), and in the process more than 3,000,000 ethnic Hungarians were absorbed into these countries. Anti-Semitism was brought out into the open for the first time after the defeat of the Communists and became a fact of life in inter-war Hungary. Bartók notes the beginnings of this when he cites the reasons for the dismissal of the general director of the Opera House in the autumn of 1919: he had appointed Jews to several positions, and had performed works by Jews.

Bartók spent the next twenty years in this new Hungary. Despite his involvement in the music administration of the Republic of Councils there is no evidence that he held a strong political view, and even his association with the artistic avant garde is more circumstantial than an open adoption of a position. So it is predictable that when he was attacked in the press for a lack of patriotism in his writings on Romanian folk music, he gave a painstaking, pedantic response, as if knee-jerk chauvinism could be countered by reasoned, quiet argument. His son Béla remembers that he read the newspaper every day, so he can hardly have been unaware of the politics of the inter-war years.

Part of the reason for Bartók's tolerance must be that he could not bring himself to leave the things he loved. First of all there was his mother, who was still living in Pozsony, now Bratislava, behind the Czechoslovakian border. Then there was his folk-song work, which, however widely he may have travelled outside eastern Europe, was concerned above all with the music of the country of his upbringing. His work on this material could only ever be properly understood in his native country. There was his friendship with Zoltán and Emma Kodály, who had no intention of leaving Hungary, and indeed remained there for the rest of their lives (Emma Kodály died in 1958 and her husband in 1967). Bartók, whether he liked it or not, was tied

Left, 'Noise', 1920. Collage by Lajos Kassák, a leading figure in the Hungarian avant garde, founder of the art journals A Tett and MA. Like Berény, Kassák left Hungary when the Republic of Councils disintegrated, and did not return until 1926.

to Budapest. Another reason why Bartók may not have felt the need to emigrate is that in the 1920s he began to achieve fame as a pianist and composer on an international level. This must have protected him, as it did Dohnányi, from the wrath of the new government. At the Academy, Hubay was keen to have the support of both men, while pursuing a personal vendetta against Kodály. Bartók hoped for a special post to be created for him in recognition of his folk-music research, but in the end he returned to teaching the piano.

In February and March of 1920 he was in Berlin, involved in a number of recitals, but he remained in the city after these had come to an end, and did not return to Budapest until the beginning of April. The rumour spread that he was intending to remain in Berlin, and a letter to Buşiţia shows that he was indeed considering this option. Berlin in March 1920 was hardly in a stable condition: Wolfgang Kapp's insurrection took place in the middle of the month, and a general strike followed.

When Bartók returned to Hungary, it was to a new home. Apparently, Dohnányi drew the attention of József Lukács (father of the Marxist philosopher György) to the Bartóks' poverty. Lukács then asked Bartók if he would take an upper floor of his house, as a favour, to prevent its requisition by a government eager to punish Lukács for having a Communist son, who had been involved in a small way in the defunct governing council (György Lukács had been giving a talk on the day the Republic of Councils came into being and his audience first heard about the change in government when he announced it). The Bartóks moved into the large family home in a smart area on the Buda side of the city on 22 May 1920 and remained there for the next two years.

During this period we have a clearer idea of Bartók's thoughts on contemporary music than at any other. He began to contribute to a number of periodicals outside Hungary, reporting on concert life for *Il pianoforte* in Turin, and the *Musical Courier* in New York. Generally he wrote his pieces in Hungarian first, and they were then translated into German (on occasion by Márta); the printed versions had the German text as their source. He also agreed to write for the prestigious American journal *Musical Quarterly*, taking his beloved Liszt as his subject, and wrote on the relationship of folk music to the development of art music for *The Sackbut* in London, having been

contacted by Philip Heseltine ('Peter Warlock'). Of course the musical environment was still politically charged. A report on musical events during December 1920, covering Schoenberg's First String Quartet and Stravinsky's pre-Diaghilev *Fireworks*, was headlined 'Schönberg and Stravinsky Enter "Christian-National" Budapest Without Bloodshed' in the *Musical Courier*. While the epithets Christian and National are borrowed from the opposition far-right party which supported the reinstatement of the king, they effectively characterize the anti-Semitic, anti-Communist and chauvinistic mood of the whole of the authoritarian Horthy era.

Modern music entered a period of rationalization in the 1920s. Composers who, before the war, had been inventing the rules as they went along, now felt that the time had come to consolidate their experiments with new structures and methods. Austria may have lost a war and an empire, but it held on to its influential role in music, and the leading figure of the Viennese avant garde, Schoenberg, came up with a method in 1921 that had far-reaching consequences. This is the method of composing with twelve notes, where all twelve are arranged into a series whose contours and order are immutable. All musical material is derived from this series, by moving it up or down several notes, running it backwards, upside down and a combination of all three. Schoenberg infamously announced at the time that his discovery would guarantee the supremacy of German music for the next hundred years – a comment bound to provoke contrary positions, and sure enough the Parisian neo-classicism of Stravinsky (and the folk-derived method of Bartók) were considered the opposition.

Schoenberg's principle was rationalization on a grand scale: in theory, and later in practice, a piece of music could be constructed from numbers alone, without reference to sound. Other composers elaborated the method in different ways, and even his two pupils, Berg and Webern, achieved vastly different results with it. Schoenberg for the moment was content to take a didactic stance, and introduce the method in the context of work that in every other aspect – genre, texture, gesture and expression – was highly conventional. Neo-classical, we might say now, paradoxically.

In Bartók's writings on music from the early 1920s we can trace fairly clearly his thoughts on the Viennese principle that all twelve chromatic notes have an equal call on the modern composer and

listener. His music throughout the 1920s does not contradict this, even though it is increasingly clear that certain notes tend to become centres of focus, and so a new hierarchy emerges. Bartók may use the same group of notes as harmony and melody, or create two mutually exclusive groups from the twelve, in a manner similar to Berg's, but only in a few pieces does he follow one of Schoenberg's ground rules: like a Victorian father telling his children that they cannot have pudding until they have eaten their main course, Schoenberg insists that a note cannot be repeated or doubled until the other eleven have had a chance to be heard. His intention was to maintain equality at all costs. Bartók, who had been immersed in oral traditions and listened to thousands of instinctive musicians, could never adopt such a literate principle. His own comment on this dates from 1927–8, in the text he prepared for his lecture-recitals in the USA: 'There was a time when I thought I was approaching a species of twelve-tone music. Yet even in the works of that period the absolute tonal foundation is unmistakable.' In his essay 'The Problem of the New Music' (written for *Melos* in Berlin) he puts forward the typical evolutionary theory of the logic of atonality, and, incidentally, the case for a notation free from sharp- and flat-signs.

From his reports for the magazines abroad we know that in the summer of 1921 Bartók heard Stravinsky's *Quatre chantes russes* of 1918–19 and *Piano-Rag-music* (1919) and Schoenberg's opus 11 piano pieces (which he notes were greeted with 'polite applause'). The only music he wrote this year, the eight Improvisations on Hungarian Peasant Songs for piano, crashes together an avant-garde piano style with folk-tune material: this is the sound he would pursue over the next few years, gradually working through the implications of a method based on combining the two elements.

In March 1921 Bartók reached forty, and the birthday was celebrated in a special edition of the journal published by Universal Edition, *Musikblätter des Anbruch*, thus drawing attention to their recent signing. As well as Bartók's autobiographical note, there were articles by Egon Wellesz on the two String Quartets, and by Kodály on the piano music for children. Bartók was now once again on the teaching staff of the Academy, but studiously avoiding contact with anyone apart from his pupils. The more affable Dohnányi was inclined to fit in with the regime as Hungary settled down; Bartók,

Bartók with the violinist
Jelly Arányi (left) and her
sister Adila, in London,
March 1922, at the time
of the première of Bartók's
First Violin Sonata, written
for Jelly

in contrast, set his face against the conservative establishment,
but in silence.

In the middle of the month Rózsavölgyi published a collection
of 150 Hungarian songs from Transylvania, put together by Bartók
and Kodály, and in October Bartók completed his work on Hungarian
folk-song (*A magyar népdal*), published three years later. Otherwise
he was occupied with orchestrating the Four Pieces which he had
written (in a two-piano version) back in 1912. But he wrote no new
music that year until Jelly Arányi called to see him at the Lukács
house in October. Together with her two sisters, Jelly had tried and
failed to return from Britain to Hungary at the beginning of World
War I. Through their influential contacts (including the British Prime
Minister) they had escaped the threat of internment as enemy aliens,
and the two older sisters had married in Britain. After the war Jelly
quickly became established as a charismatic, popular violinist, and
when she visited Bartók in the autumn of 1921, he had already grasped
that arranging a recital tour with her was a way of following up the

suggestion by his British supporter Heseltine that he should come to Britain.

After a discussion in the superior surroundings of the nearby Gellért Hotel, Bartók set to work (Márta was thrilled that he was writing again), and came up with one of his most demanding pieces, for players and listeners alike, the First Violin Sonata. This is a work so packed with ideas and abrupt changes of direction and manner that the structure seems on the point of collapse.

In February of the next year the Sonata had its first performance (not by Jelly) in Vienna; a week later Bartók's concert career began in earnest, with a two-week tour of Transylvania, followed by trips to Britain and France, organized with the help of the Arányis. The fairly reasonable, open-minded response in the foreign press to his first appearances playing his own music was in contrast to what he had met in Budapest in January, when two orchestral works had been played within a fortnight of each other. The première on 9 January of his Four Orchestral Pieces (in reality a work from 1912) was compared unfavourably in the press with his fifteen-year-old Suite No. 2, performed on the 21st. This sort of comparison was going to become typical of the way his music was viewed in his home country.

On the concert tour of Britain Bartók was drawn into the private music-making of the country, as well as the public. His accommodation in London, for example, was not the hotel room of the travelling soloist, but the home of a supporter. His first appearance, at the Mayfair home of the Hungarian chargé d'affaires, fell into the category of the society invitation concert, and the second was a concert organized by University College of Wales at Aberystwyth. He returned to London for his first public recital, in the Aeolian Hall on 24 March. The programme included two items for Jelly, the Mozart Violin Sonata, K. 306, and the Bartók Sonata, and four of the Eight Hungarian Folk-songs, sung by Grace Crawford. Otherwise Bartók's solo pieces consisted of the Suite Op. 14, and the Improvisations, two pieces by Kodály, one Burlesque and one Romanian Dance. The tone of the reviews, however mixed, reflects the eager interest in contemporary music in Britain at the time. The advocacy of Bartók's supporters did the groundwork, but the 'society' connections and presumably the appeal of Jelly Arányi (and the work of her agent) did

the rest. It is probably with this tour that Bartók was elevated into the front rank of contemporary composers in the British musical mind.

In April Bartók and Jelly took the same programme to Paris. She remembered that the leading composers of the day were in the audience, and they had a chance to meet them at a dinner afterwards. Ravel, Stravinsky, Szymanowski, Roussel, and all 'Les Six' – Honegger, Milhaud, Poulenc, Auric, Tailleferre and Durey – were reportedly there. Bartók spent some time with Stravinsky during this visit; although in 1958 Stravinsky recollected that he met Bartók in London, Bartók in the 1940s remembered their meeting in Paris. It was at this time that Bartók's opinion of Stravinsky's new aesthetic directions started to decline. He had already recognized that of the new movements in music, only in Stravinsky's was the Wagner experience irrelevant, and the spare, acidic quality of Stravinsky's unceasingly ritualized music at first appealed to him. Yet, in 1926 he told Dezső Kosztolányi that he was not moved by Stravinsky's later works. But then Stravinsky did not want anyone to be 'moved' by them.

While it can easily be imagined that Bartók separated the music from the man, it is also feasible that Stravinsky's personality had something to do with Bartók's retreat. Stravinsky's ego had long before been commented on by his first Parisian champions: Debussy characterized him as a child jealous of his toys as far back as 1913, and perhaps by the 1920s Stravinsky's strong sense of his own importance was too much for Bartók to bear.

But neo-classicism was in the air, and for Bartók the equivalent backward glance prompted a reassessment of the *verbunkos* form and idiom, an element that would have an important influence on the way his music developed. The first indication of this is the Second Sonata for violin, written between July and November 1922, and dedicated to Jelly, although Imre Waldbauer gave the first performance, with Bartók at the piano, in Berlin in February 1923, during a series of concerts organized by the *Melos* crowd. As far back as the Paris trip the previous spring, Jelly had been finding her Hungarian friend somewhat irritating: in her letters to her sisters he had gone from being 'a little difficult to be with' to 'an awfully disgusting character' in less than a week. Presumably he made a pass at her, and it was some time before she overcame her antipathy and he was invited back to Britain. Finally she played both sonatas together in London in May 1923 with Bartók at the piano, and this time 'he behaved completely correctly.'

The Second Sonata is a more relaxed piece than the first, an example of how the *verbunkos* tradition was re-entering Bartók's vocabulary: Bartók had observed *verbunkos* elements (considered products of an alien culture) being absorbed into the oral tradition and so could regard the style as a legitimate source of material. True to the form, the Second Sonata is a pair of moderate and fast movements; in the first, a rhapsodic opening theme binds the structure together, pointing the way to the shape of his next piece, the *Dance Suite*. What the two sonatas have in common, apart from being Bartók's last works with opus numbers, is an openly expressive, if not expressionistic character, lurching from the feverishly animated to the elegiac, wrapped up in formal ambiguity and puzzling tonality. There is a fascinating recording of the work played by Bartók and Szigeti in 1940, interestingly programmed with Beethoven's 'Kreutzer' sonata and Debussy's Violin Sonata.

Poster for a Bartók recital at the Budapest Academy of Music in 1923. The ticket prices (1,000 to 10,000 crowns) are evidence of the current hyper-inflation.

Ventures similar to the defunct UMZE were a feature of musical life after the war. Makers of contemporary music, now accustomed to

ZENEMŰVÉSZETI FŐISKOLA   Kedden, november 6-án este fél 9 órakor

Bartók Béla
ZONGORAESTJE

Jegyek **1000-10000** k-ig vigalmi és forgalmi adóval együtt **FODOR HANGVERSENYIRODÁBAN** IV. Váczi-utca 1 (könyvkereskedés) Telefon: **88-61** kaphatók.

Bartók with his second wife,
Ditta Pásztory, in 1923, the
year of their marriage

the rejection of conventional audiences, took matters into their own hands with far more lasting success than before. Schoenberg founded his *Verein für Musikalische Privataufführungen* ('Association for private musical performances') in 1918 (early Bartók pieces were heard under its auspices) and in 1923 an International Society for Contemporary Music (ISCM) came into being, the result of a festival of new music the year before. Based in London, it began to promote annual events in Europe, as well as sponsoring competitions.

Bartók was not happy to crusade for modern music in any other way than by composing and performing: he served on the jury of an ISCM competition in 1924, but wrote that he would have to resign if any earning engagements came up, and in any case, he would prefer to give his judgements by post. For all his involvement with the ISCM, and receipt of a commission (the Sonata for Two Pianos and Percussion in 1937), Bartók was still a figure in mainstream musical life. His prominence as a performer, probably at its peak in the late 1920s, ensured that his music was widely heard. And, as always, his programmes enticed his audience with Mozart, Beethoven and others, with rather bitty choices from his own work in between.

The Bartóks' marriage came to a sudden end in the summer of 1923. It is easily assumed from Jelly Arányi's sudden revulsion that he was still attracted to much younger, vivacious women, and indeed a relationship had started with a twenty-year-old pupil at the Academy, Ditta Pásztory. In August Béla was at Radvány in the north of Hungary, finishing his *Dance Suite*, when Márta visited him with

their son, and a divorce was agreed. 'I believe it will be better than up to now,' he wrote to his mother. 'Only to Márta it will be far worse; this is the only thing that saddens me … But she persuaded me to this change, and I could not say no; after all, I was not the only one to be considered. Little Béla accepted the situation readily enough …' So the marriage ended with the same secret formality with which it had begun.

Bartók married the glamorous Ditta in Budapest at the end of August; they set up home in the same flat which he had rented the previous year with Márta, on a square facing the Danube just below the castle district on the Buda side. Márta left with her son for Szöllős puszta where Elza now lived. Ditta eventually became her husband's partner in a piano duo, but she was never as involved in the preparation of Bartók's scores as Márta had been. Rather more mysterious and diffident than her predecessor, Ditta can be seen in photographs observing her husband with a rapt devotion that suggests she readily adapted to his needs and desires.

The orchestral work Bartók was finishing at the time was the contribution he had been asked to make to the celebrations surrounding the fiftieth anniversary of the unification of the various

Extract from Bartók's short score of the *Dance Suite*, 1923. The passage shown comes from the finale.

cities that make up Budapest. It is an indication of the 'pardon' that had been offered to the miscreants of the revolutionary period that the other composers to be commissioned were Kodály and Dohnányi. The concert, given on 19 November in the splendid surroundings of the Vigadó concert hall, opened with three first performances: Dohnányi's Festival Overture, Kodály's *Psalmus Hungaricus*, and Bartók's *Tánc-Suite*.

The *Dance Suite* is one of those works that seems to show an artist finally understanding what he should be doing: the tensions within the material are at last resolved, and he pulls back from repeating what has been over-ambitious in previous work. A simple and intelligible form is the means and a clear presentation of ideas the content. As a result, such pieces rapidly become popular, and this was the case with the *Dance Suite*, which soon appeared on concert programmes in Germany, and within two years in the USA, through the advocacy of the Hungarian-American conductor Fritz Reiner.

There are six dances, punctuated by a nostalgic refrain. The folk sources are telescoped (Arab melody with European rhythm), or

Bartók with his two sons, Béla and Péter

merely imitated (the fourth, home-made Arabian dance). Bartók has
retained only what is worthwhile in his previous orchestral works –
their confidence and energy – but the sound has been completely
cleaned up, effects are spotlighted one by one, and the brass come
into their own as an independent, boisterous family group.

Bartók was forty-two when he wrote this work. It made him a key
player in contemporary music, an example of a composer of integrity,
from a folk-song school of the non-pastoral variety. His writings on
folk music were being published outside the areas they referred to:
a book on Romanian music from Maramures was published in
German in Munich in 1923, and *The Hungarian Folk-Song* was also
published in Germany a year after its Hungarian edition (an English
edition followed six years later). Bartók's income improved, with his
salary from the Academy supplemented by recital fees, and if the
reactionary politics of Hungary between the wars was obnoxious,
it probably seemed in the 1920s to be no worse than the regime in
government before and during World War I. Bartók became a father
for the second time when Ditta gave birth to a son, Péter, in July 1924.

Bartók's only composition from that year was *Falun*, a collection of
five Slovakian songs from Zólyom county, for female voice and piano,
subtitled (in Slovakian) *Three Village Scenes*. Two years passed before
the first performance, given by the contralto Mária Basilides, a singer
who worked closely with Bartók and Kodály, frequently performing
their original vocal works as well as their folk-song arrangements. In
the meantime Bartók transcribed three of the songs for a small group
of women's voices and orchestra, and in this version the work was first
heard in New York in November 1926, conducted by Koussevitzky.
Stravinsky's *Les Noces*, in its final, 1923, orchestration for four pianos
and percussion is what the listener is inescapably reminded of by
Bartók's orchestration of the first song, 'Svatba' (Wedding) – all rat-
tling percussion and tolling bell effects. The middle lullaby is a piece
of great beauty and simplicity, with that melodic, affecting Bartókian
quality which Stravinsky was not interested in pursuing. The work
ends with the customary cheery dance.

In April 1926 Bartók at last finished his collection of Romanian
Christmas songs (*Colinde*) for publication. His negotiations to
have the material published in Bucharest came to nothing, and

The contralto Mária
Basilides, who performed
regularly with Bartók in the
inter-war years and
recorded four of the Eight
Hungarian Folk-Songs,
Sz 64, with him

Above, Bartók with Ditta, Elza and the two-year-old Péter at Elza's family home in Szöllős puszta, summer 1926. The sounds of the Szöllős puszta countryside at night inspired 'The Night's Music' movement of the piano suite *Out of Doors*. *Right*, poster for Bartók's 1926 concert in Berlin, playing the First Rhapsody for piano with the Berlin Philharmonic under Bruno Walter.

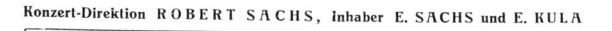

Konzert-Direktion ROBERT SACHS, Inhaber E. SACHS und E. KULA

Bernburger Str. 22 PHILHARMONIE Bernburger Str. 22

Montag, den 18. Januar 1926, abends $7^1/_2$ Uhr

III. BRUNO WALTER

Konzert mit dem **Philharmonischen Orchester**

Solist: **Béla Bartók**

1. Symphonie Nr. IX, C-moll . . . . Haydn
   Allegro
   Andante cantabile
   Menuetto
   Finale. Vivace

2. Rhapsodie für Klavier und Orchester op. 1   Béla Bartók

3. Symphonie Nr. VII, A-dur, op. 92 . . . . Beethoven
   Poco sostenuto — Vivace
   Allegretto
   Presto
   Allegro con brio

Konzertflügel: **IBACH**

Aus dem Ibach-Hause, Berlin, Steglitzer Str. 27 — Potsdamer Str. 29

IV. BRUNO WALTER

Konzert mit dem **Philharmonischen Orchester**

Mozart: Requiem

PHILHARMONIE: Montag, den 8. Februar 1926, abends $7^1/_2$ Uhr
Oeffentliche Hauptprobe: Sonntag, den 7. Februar 1926, vormittags $11^1/_2$ Uhr
Kittel'scher Chor, Lotte Leonard, Fritz Krauss etc.

eventually Universal Edition published the collection in 1935, at Bartók's own expense.

In the same year Bartók had another of those bursts of creativity after a long period of writing very little, and in the space of a few months he created a huge body of piano music. In June he wrote the Sonata, followed immediately by the suite *Szabadban* ('Out of Doors'). The titles of the individual pieces in the suite may refer to earlier keyboard styles ('Musettes', or 'Barcarolla'), but the sound world is quite new: 'With Drums and Pipes' begins with punching at the bottom of the keyboard that borders on self-parody, although this is later balanced by long legato lines of typically Bartókian melody. The 'Barcarolla' has a simple texture of contrasting elements, held octaves, a walking melodic line, and isolated rapid tapping notes. The fourth movement of the suite, dedicated to Ditta, introduces a genre piece which Bartók would explore repeatedly in later works. Only here does he make it clear from the title what his subject is: 'Az éjszaka zenéje', the night's music. It is night music of the naturalist's imagination, with the secret, miniature sounds of nature at work in the darkness. 'The Chase' is a return to the sound of *The Miraculous Mandarin*, in its original state for piano, the right hand bashing energetically over the perpetual motion of rolling chords.

Together with the Sonata, and above all, the Piano Concerto which he finished in November, the bulk of the suite uses the piano in a way which Bartók made his own at this time, generally held to be relentlessly and painfully percussive, and which was much criticized. Yet the piano textures are more three-dimensional than the criticism suggests: not only in the landscape of the night's music (felt but unseen), but also in the Sonata there is an orchestral roundness to the sound and a striking sense of space in the use of different piano resonances.

Bartók now had a greatly increased repertoire to take on tour, and he wrote to Ditta of how pleased he was to have new pieces to play 'instead of the eternal *Allegro barbaro*, "A Bit Drunk" [second of the Three Burlesques] and Romanian Dance'. Intriguingly, the premières of some of the new pieces took place in radio broadcasts in Budapest in December 1926, but the Piano Concerto had to wait until the following year, when Furtwängler conducted it, with Bartók at the piano, in a concert in the Frankfurt Opera House. In the same letter

Bartók en route to the USA,
December 1927

he complains of the avalanche of theorizing about the new music in periodicals, and how the weight of this has made him doubt whether he can still write. To the watchwords he quotes, 'linear, horizontal, vertical … polyphonic, homophonic' can be added the controversial neo-Baroque idiom of Stravinsky's work of the time.

As the American Bartók specialist Benjamin Suchoff has pointed out, the 1926 Piano Concerto is not immune from neo-Baroque influence. Bartók had recently made two tours of Italy, where musicians were starting to look into their musical inheritance from the sixteenth and seventeenth centuries. On coming home Bartók had himself begun to study early Italian keyboard works, by Frescobaldi, Marcello and others, and the style of the keyboard toccata, and the hammering repeated notes of an instrumental canzona were important in shaping the sound of the Piano Concerto.

If Stravinsky's new prominence as a performing musician prompted Bartók to pursue a similar career, then the example of another composer may have sparked off Bartók's next important work, his Third String Quartet. In July Bartók went on from the ISCM performances in Frankfurt to Baden-Baden, where he heard a performance of Berg's *Lyric Suite* for string quartet. There is no written evidence of what impression he took from the work, but the Quartet he wrote in September, back in Budapest, shows a new direction in his writing for strings. Bartók's work does not have the beautiful surface polish of the Berg, still less its programmatic content – passion and despair,

An American view of
Bartók: Aline Fruhaup's
1927 caricature.

and a coded message to the woman the composer was in love with. What the piece does have is a new concentration and a broad palette of Bartókian string effects. The elements which he shared with Stravinsky – irregular metres, punctuating stabbing chords on unpredictable beats – are more than ever identified as his own, absorbed into the existing polyphonic quartet idiom.

In December Bartók set out on his most ambitious recital trip, a tour of the USA, from coast to coast, beginning in New York on the 22nd of the month. He was to have played the Piano Concerto at Carnegie Hall, with Mengelberg and the New York Philharmonic, but, possibly because of lack of rehearsal time, the Rhapsody Op. 1 was substituted. Understandably, this was found 'over-rich' and 'old-fashioned'. The concerto had to wait until February, when Reiner conducted it with his Cincinnati Orchestra in New York and in their home city. Bartók's appearances in other cities were in the form of a lecture-recital. He would give a ten-minute talk (which ultimately he found boring, lacking the confidence in English to depart from the text), followed by a selection of piano works, with the most testing, the Sonata, at the centre. Sometimes there would be a singer to perform folk-song arrangements, and the last items would be from the first batch of piano music written between 1908 and 1910 – a burlesque, two 'easy pieces' ('Evening with the Székelys' and 'Bear Dance'), and *Allegro barbaro*. The caricature of Bartók the crazed modernist can hardly have been confirmed by his reserved public manner, or by his fastidious playing. He was by no means one of those European musicians able to fulfil the publicist's need for a sellable identity in the American musical scene of the time.

Bartók recorded a representative sample of his recital repertoire in Budapest in 1928 and 1929, including an *Allegro barbaro* much faster than the printed metronome mark. The unmechanical, almost romantic style of playing is arresting. The cabaret signer Vilma Medgyaszay joined him in a charming performance of five of the 1906 Hungarian Folk-songs. Bartók sketched richer, more imaginative piano accompaniments for the recording, later reconstructed by the Belgian musicologist Denijs Dille, the future director of the Budapest Bartók Archive. What Dille only gives a hint of is the rhythmic freedom and expressive imagination of Medgyaszay's singing.

Out for a walk in the snow
with Péter in Budapest, 1929

In Philadelphia at the end of December, Bartók entered the newly-finished Quartet anonymously in a competition sponsored by the city's Music Fund Society. Months later he heard that he had shared first prize of 6,000 dollars with the Italian composer Alfredo Casella. The Quartet was consequently first performed in Philadelphia in December 1928. But before he had even heard the piece, Bartók went

ahead with writing a Fourth Quartet, composed in the summer of
1928. The two works can easily be viewed as a pair, even if they com-
plement each other rather than match, and despite the fact that the
Third Quartet sounds like the end of one road and the Fourth the
beginning of another. They are quite different in the way they are
constructed. The Third is based on the *verbunkos* form, but the two
movements seem to have crashed into each other. The second movement is like a firework that has been lit too early, and when it fizzles
out the first resumes. Whatever spark the second movement has left
is attached as a rapid coda.

Bartók with the
violinist József Szigeti, in
Budapest, 1927

'Is Bartók Mad – Or Are We?' This cartoon in the *Radio Times* of 9 December 1927 accompanied Percy Scholes's article of the same name, written in the wake of Bartók's two BBC broadcasts, one of short piano pieces, the other of *Two Portraits, Dance Suite* and the First Piano Concerto.

The later quartet is an elaborate arch of five movements, with a piece of night's music at the centre. László Somfai has revealed that this famous example of a characteristic Bartók structure was actually a late decision on the part of the composer. The piece was already complete in four movements when a fifth (fourth in the final plan) was added. In the arch of the Fourth Quartet, what is cramped and unforthcoming at the beginning is open and broad at the end; within this outer shell, the chase of the second movement, where all the strings are muted, is balanced by the fourth where all the strings are plucked. Here we meet for the first time the folk-fiddle type sound now known as a Bartók pizzicato, where the string is plucked so hard it bounces off the fingerboard. At the centre is a movement of serene beauty, where the top and bottom instrumental voices, far from coming together to create the cramped textures of the earlier quartet, tumble apart: the cello sings a long, ornamented folk improvisation, and the first violin sings like a bird in the night.

The first performance of the Fourth Quartet was in a BBC broadcast from London, given by the Waldbauer Quartet in February 1929, and the same players gave the Budapest première of both works together a month later.

The other music Bartók wrote during 1928 shows a different side of his musical vision. He had begun to collaborate with the violin virtuoso József Szigeti, and wrote two Rhapsodies for violin and piano for their joint recitals. These genre pieces revive the *verbunkos* sound and form unashamedly (Kodály had just done the same in his opera *Háry János*) and their orchestrated versions include the sound of the traditional zither, the cimbalon. Nothing could be more approachable and less like the image of the piano-basher than these two instantly appealing, melodic works.

As the 1920s drew to an end, Bartók embarked on his most con-centrated months of concert-giving. Between January and April he toured to the Soviet Union (Kharkov, Odessa, Leningrad and Moscow), Switzerland (where he first met the conductor Paul Sacher), Denmark, Germany, Britain, the Netherlands, France and Italy. He was an international name, not a Rachmaninov perhaps, but a figure of integrity and recognized as a contemporary master.

6

Four peasant women
photographed by Bartók

*For miles on end, in these parts, there are entire
villages with illiterate inhabitants, communities
which are not linked by any railways or roads;
here, most of the time the people can provide for
their own daily wants … When one comes into
such a region, one has the feeling of a return to
the Middle Ages.*

Bartók: *Romanian Folk Music* (1933)

The Clearest Springs 1930-39

As Bartók entered his fifties, his music entered a new period of poise, and the elements he had been juggling for years fell into place to form the idiom of his classic works. Of course *Bluebeard's Castle*, *Allegro barbaro*, *The Miraculous Mandarin* and *Dance Suite* are all classics of their kind, but in the 1930s Bartók had reached the point where he could produce a series of works in various genres without abruptly changing style or pausing to absorb outside influences. The irony is that he achieved this at precisely the time when the unsteady ground of a peaceful Europe began to slide unstoppably into war and destruction.

Bartók's music in the 1930s (and beyond) became increasingly serene, while circumstances outside became increasingly fraught. Béla described how his father withdrew to the quietest part of the house, and even behind a sound-proofed door to be able to compose. What Bartók wrote suggests that he was also withdrawing into a Hungary of the imagination. In this politicized decade retreat was in the air, and many artists turned back from experimentation, not just those who were directly affected by opposing ideologies of the left and right. Bartók, living in Hungary, the revolving door of Eastern Europe between Germany and the Soviet Union, was not inspired by either ideology, nor was he at home with the tawdry nationalism of Horthy's Hungary.

Because the works of the 1930s are such classics, and because they were seemingly written in reaction to the disappointments of the outside world, it is worth examining them in turn. They seem to speak far more eloquently for Bartók's interior life than any other work he produced, in words or in music.

If Bartók seems to have had more in common with the inward-looking mood of Western Europe and the USA, this was just one more contradiction in the way his life and career developed during the 1930s. Here was a man who had an international reputation, but was still earning his living as a piano teacher in Budapest, worrying

about his pension. He was a name to conjure with as a composer, and yet the initial wave of enthusiasm for his work had passed. Of course Bartók benefited from the growth of broadcasting, and from initiatives to promote contemporary music, but these did not win him an audience. The only feasible money-making activity was performing, and as a fashionable figure on the concert circuit his stock saw a definite decline in the years up until the war. His true home was in Hungary, and his overriding concern was for Hungarian folk music. But Hungary was not interested in him, his breadth of vision, or his concerns, and as for the Budapest public, he snubbed them as he snubbed everything that offended him in his native country.

From time to time throughout his career Bartók stopped composing, and even declared himself an 'ex-composer'. But the fact was that he had no doubts about his destiny, and he always returned to his calling. The difference in the 1930s was that he became more open about his self-confidence and his awareness of the position he held. He refused to play in Nazi Germany, or to have his music broadcast either there or in Fascist Italy. His professional correspondence, especially with his publishers, had often had a sulky note; now he became even more tetchy, and not just with professional colleagues. In December 1930 he commented to his mother and aunt, who had been congratulating him on his recent success in London, that it was 'about twenty-four years overdue'. His letters to Oxford University Press, as negotiations to publish his collection of Romanian Christmas songs (*Colinde*) in 1931 finally came to nothing, are written in a mood of pained exasperation.

Bartók in 1936, the year in which he composed *Music for Strings, Percussion and Celesta*

The Christmas songs had a special significance for Bartók. In 1915 he made piano arrangements of a number of them as part of his sudden flood of folk-piano writing. *Colinde* are sung at Christmas, but only a small part of their content is Christian. Mostly they contain elements of epic ballads, possibly pre-Christian in origin, and one of them especially appealed to Bartók – the story of nine brothers who spent so long hunting in the woods that they were turned into stags. When their father goes out to find his sons, he comes across the stags and takes aim to fire on them. But the largest of the stags, once his favourite son, pleads with him not to shoot, or he and his brothers will be unable to stop themselves from attacking him. The father begs them to come home: their mother is waiting, the torches are lit, the

Extract from the close of
Cantata profana, showing
the tenor soloist's
concluding line '... csak
hűvös forrásból'. Bartók's
meticulous hand-written
orchestral and vocal
scores were published by
Universal Edition.

table is laid and the goblets are full of wine. The large stag answers that they can never come home again. Their antlers will not pass through the door, they need the broad space of the valleys. Their slender bodies will never wear clothes again, they will only be seen amid the foliage; their fine feet will not stand on the hearth, only on dead leaves, and they will never drink from a glass again, only from cool mountain streams.

Bartók acquired a Hungarian translation of this oddly affecting text with the intention of making a musical setting of it, but what he eventually began to set was a new Romanian version. Then at a certain point he switched to Hungarian, and the Romanian text disappeared when the work was published. The resulting piece, written in the summer of 1930, was the cantata *A kilenc csodaszarvas*, 'The Nine Enchanted Stags', or *Cantata profana*.

This caricature appeared in the *Radio Times* of 18 May 1934, in connection with an all-Bartók concert on 25 May, consisting of *Two Portraits*, the Second Piano Concerto, and the première of *Cantata profana*.

The Latin title captures some of the composer's ideas behind the work; first of all there is a definite awareness of neo-Baroque fashions of the period in the setting – Stravinsky wrote his *Symphony of Psalms* in the same year. The Bach model is not a mere cantata, but the St Matthew Passion itself, and the beginning of the Bartók directly recalls the rolling motion of the chorus which opens the Bach. Then of course there is the mixture of the Christian and pagan which is a characteristic of the *colinda* texts. The 'profane' element in the work lies in its absorption in nature – man becomes one with the natural world and leaves civilization behind – and it has been convincingly argued that the story is a Romanian creation myth. The piece was immensely important to Bartók, and suggests that his love of nature had a spiritual dimension. While in the USA in the 1940s he made his own English translation of the text ('the first product of my career as a poet in English'), and it shows a nice grasp of an archly 'poetic' English style.

Bartók intended the work as part of a sequence, probably a trilogy, of cantatas based on folk material from Romanian, Slovakian and Hungarian sources. In the end, only this piece was written, and it was nearly four years until its first performance, by BBC forces in a radio broadcast in May 1934. The broadcast was an all-Bartók concert (the other works were the *Two Portraits* and the Second Piano Concerto). The *Radio Times* drew attention to it with an angular caricature of the composer, which has little connection with the enchanted natural world of the cantata. It may be far less performed than any other of Bartók's mature works, but it has a sureness of touch and a beauty of sound which give a foretaste of the very last works.

The three movements of the cantata, which all run together, are in clearly defined sections, according to the narrative. In the first movement the chorus begins to tell the tale. The hunters set off with a noisy, boisterous fugue, but when they cross a bridge and turn into stags, Bartók conveys the magic of the moment with a simple, eerie effect of abrupt swooping up and down the harp strings. In the second movement, with the chorus still narrating, the father (a bass) confronts his favourite son (a tenor). Harp sweeps precede each of the son's comments, as if to herald a communication from another world, and the tenor's anguished lines contrast strongly with the steady sad pleading of the bass. The resigned third movement goes back over the

story, and ends with an echo of the son's last words: a beautiful melisma on '… csak hűvös forrásbol' ('… only from cool springs'). This arching phrase uses the notes of Bartók's acoustic scale, his discovery of twenty years before.

A recent model for Bartók's work may have been Kodály's *Psalmus Hungaricus*, also written for chorus and orchestra, with a tenor solo. The narrative of the Bartók piece is similarly led by the chorus, each choral line entering in turn, mostly with one note to a syllable; only the solo voices are allowed to be more expansive. The first concert performance of *Canata profana* was given in London two years after the broadcast, again by BBC forces, under Adrian Boult.

Bartók's inclusive nationalism, which could lead him to write music not only inspired by a Romanian story, but setting Romanian words, and to plan accompanying Slovak and Hungarian pieces, naturally led him into distasteful controversy not only in Hungary, but in the surrounding countries. In January 1931 he wrote a long letter to the Romanian folklorist Octavian Beu correcting various points which Beu had covered in a draft text of a radio talk on Bartók. The composer is at pains to point out what in his work has a Romanian source and what has not. He makes the following telling, if idealistic statements:

> *My creative work, just because it arises from three sources (Hungarian, Romanian, Slovakian), might be regarded as the embodiment of the very concept of integrity so emphasized in Hungary today … My own idea, however – of which I have been fully conscious since I found myself as a composer – is the brotherhood of peoples, brotherhood in spite of all wars and conflicts.*

The integrity which Bartók refers to was of course simple political revisionism, a longing for the restoration of those parts of Hungary lost under the Treaty of Trianon. In the circumstances it would have been provocative to perform the *Cantata profana* in Budapest at this time. The first performance there was not given until 1936, conducted by Dohnányi: he was no longer a hero of Bartók's while he remained in favour with the regime, and Bartók described their relationship as 'chilly'.

Bartók himself was loath to perform his own music in the city during the 1930s, and equally unwilling to acknowledge the political

In the 1930s, under Horthy's regency, Hungarian politics moved even further to the right.

establishment. His status as a refusenik is clear from the way he responded in 1931 to the award of a Corvin Medal, a new decoration instituted by Horthy, and awarded by the Regent in person. Bartók simply did not turn up for the ceremony, as his pupil Andor Földes remembered. There was a comment in the press that Bartók did not receive the award in person because he was abroad, but in fact he was sitting at home in Budapest. He did, however, go to the French Embassy a few days earlier to receive his Légion d'honneur, although he commented that, instead of the award, he would have preferred more performances of his music in Paris.

Folklore and its use was becoming controversial; not only was there the tension in the Danube basin, but the rise of National Socialism had a folk-song aspect, and Schoenberg's scathing article on 'Folk Symphonies', where, without naming names, he dismisses the work

The Bartók family at home in Csalán út, early 1930s. Bartók grew a moustache while illness kept him at home.

of composers who use folk material, springs from such developments. (It is unlikely that Schoenberg, so completely a product of the Austro-German tradition, could grasp what it was that Bartók found in folk music.) The public stance of artists and musicians in the face of the right-wing advance across Europe was never more keenly observed. In 1931 Toscanini conducted a concert in honour of the Italian composer Martucci in Bologna. As always, he refused to play the Fascist anthem before the concert began, and consequently was set upon by Fascist party members. Throughout the 1930s Toscanini was a beacon of resistance in musical circles to the regimes in his home country, Germany, and finally Austria. This was the matter that most exercised Bartók's mind when he went to Geneva to serve on the International Committee of Intellectual Co-operation, a committee of the League of Nations, in July of that year. He had already formulated a 'draft resolution' on behalf of a resurrected UMZE, in protest against the treatment of Toscanini in May.

Bartók reports on the doings of the International Committee in the rather wry tone of the detached observer. Nevertheless he was

prepared to speak up on the topic of international co-operation when it came to sharing folk material for study. He took part in the Cairo International Congress of Arab Music in the spring of 1932, in the company of the German composer Paul Hindemith and the Austrian composer and musicologist Egon Wellesz (an expert on Byzantine music). He also taught piano and composition – in spite of the poor attendance of pupils – at an Austro-American summer school in Austria, after the Geneva trip. But Bartók did not undergo any personality change through his involvement in all this public work. He was not seduced by the glamour of international conferences into being anything other than what he was: hard-working, honest, unexpansive, with his famously piercing eyes trained only on what was essential. There was no frivolity or self-indulgence in the Bartók family, but Béla has dismissed the charge that his father lacked a sense of humour. In fact Bartók was devoted to the sort of items once to be found in 'joke shops'.

The music of the 1930s communicates the most deeply-felt emotions. After the *Cantata* came a second, immediately appealing Piano Concerto, composed first of all in a two-piano version in the autumn of 1930, and orchestrated the following year. This is a noisy, punchy work, more melodic than the first, and structurally an example of the arch shape which, after the Fourth Quartet, was becoming Bartók's regular choice of construction. The constantly cadencing Brandenburgish ritornello of the first movement, with its four-square rhythm, is transformed into the fluid, rolling motto of the last, and the slow central movement has a furious piano Scherzo at its heart, with calm, chorale-like chords for strings on either side. Even with new element of neo-Baroque gestures the sound-world retains the Bartók characteristics of brass fanfares and the coupling of piano and timpani. The first performance was in Frankfurt in January 1933; Bartók played the solo and Hans Rosbaud conducted. This was the last time Bartók appeared in Germany.

The idea of producing *The Miraculous Mandarin* at the Opera House in Budapest was once again floated, but came to nothing. Bartók undertook to pass on any royalties for the other two stage works to Balázs, who was living abroad, to allow performances of the opera and ballet to go ahead, but even these did not take place until 1936. He returned to educational music in 1931, after the German

Bartók in a radio studio in
Budapest in the mid-1930s
violin teacher Erich Doflein contacted him proposing to make an
arrangement of *For Children* for violins. Not long before, Szigeti had
arranged seven *For Children* pieces for violin and piano (he and the
composer recorded them in 1930). Bartók instead wrote new pieces
for learners, the folk-based Forty-four Duos. The sound of two violins
in these short pieces is unavoidably more authentically folkish than
the piano-folk music can ever be, and the sources reflect the far wider
experience of folk cultures that Bartók now had, in comparison with
the days of *For Children.*

The collapse of the western economies was signalled by the Wall
Street Crash of October 1929, but it took some time before its effects
were felt in Hungary. Two years later the Hungarian banks failed, as
they did in Germany and Austria. The country's economy had already
been organized through the intervention of the League of Nations in

the 1920s, putting an end to a period of hyperinflation, and once again the country appealed to the League for help. The remedies proposed by France and carried out by a new government managed to alienate precisely those groups in Hungary, nationalist, revisionist and anti-Semitic, who were the equivalent of the growing radical right in Germany and Austria. Not much more than a year later, in October 1932, a new right-wing Party of National Unity, led by Gyula Gömbös, came into power, with all the necessary trappings of a government-controlled press and a propaganda office. Any swing back to more liberal policies when the economy was in better shape was dealt with by Gömbös's dictatorial actions (he intended to introduce a one-party state), and when he died suddenly in 1936, the country was too strongly allied to Hitler's Germany for there to be any hope of change.

Bartók's country and the city that had been his home for so many years was becoming enemy territory. His first reaction was to retreat, and in April 1932 he and his family moved out from the city to a house in the middle-class suburbs of the Buda hills. This is the house in Csalán út which is now a museum to the composer. So completely was he settled there that for the short time that he was still employed by the Academy, he asked his pupils on occasion to come out to the house for their lessons. Just as in the classroom there were two pianos together in the largest room, while upstairs Bartók had

The Csalán út house where Bartók lived in the 1930s is now a museum, and Imre Varga's statue of the composer stands in the garden.

a separate study. The spaciousness and quiet location of the house, set amid trees, next to an empty site, gave the perfect conditions for Bartók to compose. Béla was now living with his father and family, studying engineering in Budapest, while his half-brother Péter was still only at primary school.

Bartók was in demand as a writer on music more than ever before. In 1931, for instance, he contributed three articles for a Hungarian reference work, and three more for a Budapest journal *Új Idők* ('New Times'), as well as writing on the tired controversy of 'Gypsy Music or Hungarian Music?' for *Ethnographia*. In this article Bartók berates a certain German editor of a collection of Hungarian songs for preferring those songs which betray the characteristics of popular gypsy music. As sensitively as he can, Bartók makes his point about the inadmissibility of gypsy music as Hungarian music: folk cultures do exist among gypsy groups; the point that he and Kodály had been trying to make is that the nineteenth-century idea of equating Hungarian gypsy music with Hungarian folk music is not valid. In this article too, Bartók makes a definite distinction between peasant music ('all the tunes which endure among the peasant class of any nation, in a more or less wide area and for a more or less long period') and folk music ('no one has yet told us what folk music is'). It is surely in the light of the political uses of folk culture that Bartók now chose to distinguish the two terms.

In February 1934 Bartók studied recordings of Romanian folk material at the Bucharest Gramophone Archives.

The academic objectivity of Bartók's approach was unfortunately a small voice in the angry 1930s, when a political stance could be entirely based on mutual distrust of neighbours and notions of ethnic superiority. The controversy surrounding the creation of a memorial plaque on the house in Sînnicolau Mare where Bartók was born is a case in point. Originally mooted in 1931, at the time of his fiftieth birthday, and then abandoned, it was revived three years later when Bartók planned a trip to Romania, and the temporary refusal of an entry permit was overturned by the intervention of two Romanian musicians: the violinist and composer George Enescu and the folk-lorist Constantin Brăiloiu. But Bartók was not allowed to travel to Sînnicolau Mare and the plaque idea was once again shelved.

In the summer of 1934 Bartók finally managed to negotiate an end to his teaching and his acceptance into the folk-music department of the Hungarian Academy of Sciences. At last he was set free from the

demands of a job he had finally tired of, and was able to work on
transcribing and cataloguing the recorded material which had been
deposited there over the years. His inaugural address as a member
of the Academy, however, was not on folk music at all, but on Liszt.
As well as appearing in the Academy's periodical, his talk was printed
in *Nyugat*.

The American patroness of contemporary music Elisabeth Sprague
Coolidge commissioned a String Quartet from Bartók in 1934,
and he worked on the piece that summer, finishing it in September.
Although structured in the same way as the Fourth (but with one
Scherzo in the middle and two slow movements on either side),
this is a much more expansive work. The cramped chromatic shapes
have given way to larger intervals, longer melodic lines and a powerful energy that really does prompt the often-quoted comparison with
Beethoven's late quartets. The work looks forward as well as back:
while there is a Beethoven-like sense of elaboration and variation
of the musical material, much of the string writing looks forward to
the music of Lutosławski in the 1960s.

Bartók's own analysis of the work makes specific reference to the
conventional pillars of harmonic structure – a revealing and useful
starting point for analysis not only of this work, but previous ones as
well. The Scherzo, 'alla Bulgarese', introduces the phenomenon of the
'so-called Bulgarian rhythm' which Bartók would return to at the end
of the his educational *Mikrokosmos* pieces for piano, and which he

Recital by Bartók and the
violinist Imre Waldbauer
in the concert hall of the
Budapest Academy of
Music, 12 January 1934

Top, Bartók visited   in the Museum of
Stockholm in April 1934   Musical History, playing
to play the Second Piano   a hurdy gurdy.
Concerto under Václav   *Above, Bartók at the piano,*
Talich. He is pictured here *at home in Csalán út, 1936*

discussed in the Budapest journal *Énekszó* ('The Sung Word') in May 1938. These are metres of uneven rhythm, made up in a variety of ways, from a simple 2+3, or 2+2+3 to longer groupings; the Scherzo in the Fifth Quartet starts in a metre of 4+2+3. In fact Bartók discovered that these rhythms were not peculiar to Bulgaria: they also occur in some Romanian music and further south in what he describes as the Serbo-Croatian language area. But while such fluid rhythms have been well preserved in Bulgarian peasant music, this is not the most striking aspect of it: there are often grating (to the Western ear) harmonies, sung in an open, rasping timbre for maximum effect.

In 1935 Bartók had plans to travel to Bulgaria on a recital tour, and hoped to hear Bulgarian peasants singing for himself. A surviving letter on the subject is rather opaque in giving the reasons for cancellation: 'because of a breach of faith on the part of the Antonov Concert Agency', but is interesting in that it shows Bartók asking a contact in Sofia (a folklorist) for books to help him learn Bulgarian. His dedication to learning languages is remarked on by many of his colleagues, although Kodály made the rather sour comment that Bartók had no real gift for languages. As well as his knowledge of the languages spoken in pre-Trianon Hungary (and of course, the Western European languages) Bartók would have come into constant contact with dialects not only during his field trips, but when he came to transcribe the song texts.

There are two sets of choral folk-song arrangements from the mid-1930s, which bring Bartók's work in this vein to an end. Both sets are for unaccompanied choruses: the Twenty-seven Choruses for children and women, and *Elmúlt időkből* ('From Olden Times') for men. These are elaborate arrangements: *From Olden Times* has the usual repertoire of effects found in choral singing, imitative entries, word-painting and the like. So although Bartók is far away from the folkloristic salon-song of the turn of the century, he is still involved in making arrangements for literate, if amateur musicians, and the sound-world they tend to inhabit is the mannered, careful one of the choral society, not the spontaneous, rough-hewn one of the peasant singer. Nevertheless, Bartók was pleased when he heard schoolchildren performing his choruses with a style of delivery close to the peasant sound. These choral pieces quickly became popular, but inevitably

there was a political dimension to their popularity. They stray into territory more easily associated with Kodály and his work in reviving a Hungarian choral tradition in the Singing Youth movement.

After these works, the stage was set for Bartók's last European compositions, not one of which was premièred in Hungary. Bartók was by now completely alienated from the Hungarian establishment, as one event from the end of 1935 makes plain. The conservative literary association, the Kisfaludy Society, was in the habit of award-ing annual prizes for new work in the arts. Years before, Bartók and Kodály had applied to the society for financial help in the work of transcribing and cataloguing the growing collection of folk materials. Six artistic areas were rotated, and a prize, the Greguss Medal, was due for composition in 1935, in recognition of music written during the previous six years. It seems that Bartók's name was put forward by a well-meaning critic, and that the First Orchestral Suite, which had been performed not long before, was nominated because the style would not offend the Society. When Bartók read about the award he immediately despatched a letter to the Society, pointing out the date of the piece (1905), which made it ineligible, recommending other worthier pieces by Kodály (like the *Dances of Galánta*), and finishing: 'In conclusion may I declare that I do not wish to accept the Greguss Medal in the present or in the future, neither alive nor dead.'

An offer of a commission, the first of three, came in early 1936 when Paul Sacher, founder and conductor of the Basle Chamber Orchestra, contacted Bartók. Sacher's commitment to new music resulted in the creation of an impressive number of twentieth-century classics, including works by Stravinsky, Strauss and Hindemith. Bartók's commissions from the Basle group strengthened his connec-tions with a city he had first visited as part of his extensive touring in the first months of 1929. During the later 1930s he was in correspond-ence with a certain Frau Müller-Widmann, the wife of a Basle doctor. Not only was the couple's house a base for him while touring during these years, but it also became the temporary posting-station for his manuscripts when he began to transfer them out of Hungary in 1938.

The piece which Bartók wrote for Sacher's orchestra is the four-movement *Music for Strings, Percussion and Celesta* – a clumsy title perhaps, but one which reflects the originality of the work's structure

The audience stands for the national anthem as Horthy and his family enter the royal box at the Budapest Opera House in 1935

Bartók in Switzerland, where he regularly took his summer holidays during the 1930s

and a sound-world that is like a musical equivalent of constructivism. The movements are in the pattern Slow-Fast-Slow-Fast, and include the familiar Bartók elements of arch form (in the third movement), a cramped, chromatic opening and a bright, extrovert close, and 'music of the night'. There is a touch of the Baroque in the antiphonal layout of two string orchestras, with percussion in the middle, but this is only one spatial element in a piece that has deep perspectives of sound, where the piano can join either the haze of celesta and harp or the piercing attack of its percussive cousin, the xylophone. Haze and clarity are opposed throughout the four movements: the first begins in an undertone, gradually grows towards a loud climax, then instantly returns to muddied, secretive textures. The second movement is bright and sharp, full of spiky, machine-like energy. The third movement is a piece of night music, but a particularly elaborate and varied one, while human joy and dancing rhythms return for the finale.

Like Bartók's following work, the Sonata for Two Pianos and Percussion, the *Music for Strings, Percussion and Celesta* has been exhaustively analysed by the Hungarian musicologist Ernő Lendvai, and with surprising results. His analyses have had such wide currency that it is worth pausing here, with a classic of both Bartók's output and Lendvai's theory, to consider in some detail just how Bartók composed.

The rationalization of methods of writing music in the early 1920s largely passed Bartók by. He was too much absorbed in the natural world of folk performance and of musical styles sanctioned by centuries of oral tradition to impose a theoretical construct on musical sounds, like Schoenberg's high-wire act of keeping all twelve notes in play without ever touching the ground of home notes or keys. Bartók's folk experience offered him a source of unfamiliar, gutsy sounds, both vigorous and plangent, and a strong sense of harmonic order. Neither of these, however, matched the neat designs of European classical music, though they did have elements in common, and Bartók's music reflects this when we hear it.

In the 1950s, when composers pursued ever more rigorous systems and formulas, Bartók was shunned by the Western avant garde. At the same time his music slipped effortlessly into the mainstream repertoire of symphony orchestras. Then Lendvai made his 'discovery': Bartók did use a system. He worked with natural phenomena, the proportions of the Golden Section, the numbers of the Fibonacci series and a linking of notes across the axes on the clock face of the circle of fifths (the arrangement in a circle, going up clockwise an interval of five notes at a time, of all twelve notes). This circle is the net

The diagram of the circle of fifths from Heinichen's 1728 treatise, *Der Generalbaß in der Composition.* Relative minor ('moll') keys are placed adjacent to the major ('dur'), so the interval of a fifth is between each alternate segment.

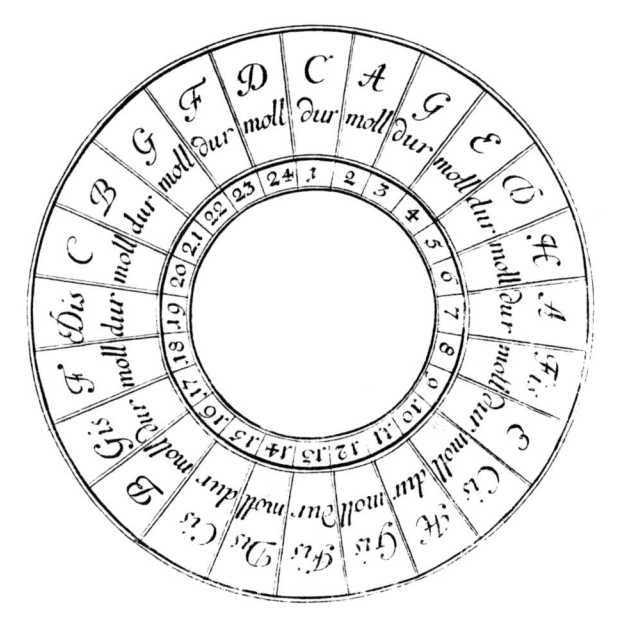

supporting Baroque music first described in a treatise by the German composer Heinichen in 1728; every time we hear a pattern of phrases, in a Vivaldi piece, for instance, climb securely through various keys, it is the order in this circle which is being followed. Bartók apparently chose to link the poles, making three groups of four notes.

The opening fugue of the *Music for Strings, Percussion and Celesta* seems to illustrate all Lendvai's points: a quietly turning chromatic theme begins on A (at twelve o'clock), and each new entry is alternately at a fifth above and a fifth below – one o'clock, eleven o'clock, and so on. Logically the entries will meet at six o'clock (E flat), and indeed the movement climaxes on insistent, pulsing E flats. This climax happens to be around the fifty-fifth bar of an approximate total of eighty-nine. The proportions of adjacent numbers in the Fibonacci number sequence (1, 1, 2, 3, 5, 8, 13 etc.), become increasingly close to that of the Golden Section, and fifty-five and eighty-nine are two such adjacent numbers.

For Lendvai, this is the development of what was hinted at in the irregular numbers of bars of galloping chords in *Allegro barbaro* years before. On the debit side, there is the problem that the time-signature of the fugue is constantly changing, so hardly two bars in succession are of the same length; the fifty-fifth bar is consequently not a very exact Golden Section. Nor is there any written evidence from Bartók that he worked out such numerical devices, or any trace on the sketches of the proportions being assembled. It is possible that Lendvai is simply fixing in detail what Bartók could create instinctively. Yet other aspects of Lendvai's theorizing do seem to account for the sound Bartók makes, in the chords which he habitually constructs. As always, the key to Bartók's method is the use of what is natural, like the acoustic scale of overtones, technically a 'natural' phenomenon.

The last movement of the *Music for Strings, Percussion and Celesta* is one of Bartók's most powerful and open finales: a rondo of unstoppable energy, from the straight-up-and-down first theme onwards. As the folk tunes disintegrate and the tempo is wound up, the first movement fugue theme solemnly returns, opened out and clarified, in an almost theatrical gesture. There is a moment of quiet expectation, the speed picks up again, and the music escalates to a climax on a daring use of a nineteenth-century cliché: a diminished seventh chord – the sort of musical effect we associate with a driver-

Budapest, den 6. Dez. 1937.

Sehr geehrte Frau Rossat!

Für Brüssel schlage ich folgende meiner Klavierstücke vor:

- 3. Suite, op. 14   10'
- 4. Allegro barbaro   2
- 2. Musiques nocturnes   5'
- 1. Preludio et All'Ungherese   3'

Jetzt möchte ich noch folgendes wissen: welche der
(Konzerte findet bei Tag (vormittag, nachmittag) statt,
öffentlichen). Wegen dem Anzug frage ich dies; die Vorlesung
ist wohl spät nachmittag, und da genügt wohl
ein dunkler Strassenanzug.*

Für eine Tournée genügt das; anfang Febr.
so ich sowieso schon in Budapest sein.
Mit den besten Grüssen Ihr ergebener
Béla Bartók

* Ich nehme an dass am 18. vormittag eine
Probe meines Orchesterwerkes in Haag stattfindet,
es wäre wünschenswert, wenn ich es vor der Aufführung
hören könnte.

The opening of the Sonata for
Two Pianos and Percussion,
written in the summer of 1937,
in Bartók's autograph

less train speeding towards a heroine tied to the rail track. This is the
four-note axis chord illustrated above, and the powerful, pregnant
effect it makes here underlines the fact that if Bartók was indeed using
a system, it could lead, paradoxically, to some familiar solutions. The
music teeters on this see-saw for a moment, and then tumbles down
to its close.

It was not long before the *Music for Strings, Percussion and Celesta*
found its home in the mainstream concert repertoire, and it remains
one of Bartók's most popular works. The Concertgebouw Orchestra's
conductor Eduard van Beinum took the piece up, and performed it
on tour in the Netherlands, a country where Bartók was a frequent
visitor in the late 1930s. The first British performance was in a BBC
concert, conducted by Hermann Scherchen, and Beecham conducted
the work in London in March 1939.

Bartók worked on his second Paul Sacher commission during the summer of 1937, while in Carinthia. This was another large-scale work, a Sonata for Two Pianos and Percussion, and the first perform-ance, in Basle the following January, was the occasion of Ditta's concert début, playing together with her husband. There is a record-ing made later in the USA of the couple playing the work – fascinating to hear if not as accurate as modern performances. The Sonata is like a distillation of the experiments carried out in the *Music for Strings, Percussion and Celesta*: the same principles are at work, and the same aesthetic, but the sound is the black-and-white one of piano and percussion. Mechanical timpani make an essential contribution to the skin-and-bone sound, as they rumble up and down between notes; at the opposite end of this monochrome spectrum is the bright hardness of the xylophone, which acts both as a melody instrument (in the last movement) and the voice of the key moments in the structure (the climax of the first movement).

There was no lack of performances of the new work, with Béla and Ditta playing the piece on Luxembourg Radio and in London for an ISCM Festival, before the Budapest première in October. It is charac-teristic of Bartók's careful approach to public performance that in case the ensemble fell apart, there was a conductor for these first perform-ances: Sacher at the première (although he wrote later that he was not needed), Scherchen again in London, and Ansermet in Budapest.

In 1932, dissatisfied with the music his son Péter was being given to play at his lessons, Bartók started to put together his largest collection of graded piano pieces for the learner, which eventually became *Mikrokosmos*. Some pieces he took from material composed in 1926, while the rest was composed throughout the 1930s. Two books were drafted, but the work was eventually published in six.

The pieces are full of character and humour, and technical points are handled with great imagination. The first sixty-six pieces are dedicated to Péter, and it is impossible to play them without being aware that they were written by a father for a small boy. As the collec-tion advances, the pieces became much more demanding. The very last six pieces, all ebullient 'Dances in Bulgarian Rhythm', were dedi-cated to the British pianist Harriet Cohen when the collection was published in 1940. Bartók performed a number of the *Mikrokosmos* pieces, not only solo, but in two-piano arrangements made expressly

Sketch of Bartók at the piano
by George Buday, 1938

for Ditta and himself, of 'New Hungarian Song' (Book 5) and
'Bulgarian Dance' (Book 4) for example.

The Europe which the composer and his wife were touring in
1938 was changing rapidly. Bartók's letters are full of scornful references to Nazi Germany: in one instance he could not bring himself
to write the word Germany and referred to it only with a drawing of
a swastika. The annexation of Austria in March of that year had
immediate consequences for him: the Austrian performing right
association which he belonged to was immediately swallowed up by
the Germany society STAGMA, and like all composers registered he
was sent a questionnaire to establish his 'Aryan' credentials. Bartók
understood that even to reply facetiously to this nonsense was in effect

to recognize the questionnaire. He began a long process of negotiating membership of the British Performing Right Society, which he eventually achieved.

Universal Edition was also cleared of anything unacceptable to the Nazis, and its directors dismissed. Ralph Hawkes, the expansionist director of the London- and New York-based music publisher Boosey and Hawkes, saw the opportunity to add Bartók and Kodály to their list. Bartók agreed, and all his works from the Sonata for Two Pianos onwards were taken by the company. Universal Edition released him from his contract, although they did not release the rights to earlier, published works, but Boosey and Hawkes did obtain the *Mikrokosmos* pieces which were being prepared at UE. Music editors who had been thrown out of UE, among them Erwin Stein, who had been working on Bartók's works, went to London and New York to join Boosey and Hawkes.

Bartók was meanwhile working on a piece in the more conventional genre of a solo concerto. It was commissioned by the violinist Zoltán Székely, a Hubay pupil, with whom Bartók had given numerous recitals, and who was the dedicatee of the Second Violin Rhapsody. It was Székely's idea that the work should be in the conventional shape of three movements; Bartók wanted to write a large variation form instead, and did so while respecting the three-movement structure. While the work was under way, a second commission came via another old friend, Szigeti, on behalf of himself and the swing clarinettist Benny Goodman (who was to pay for the piece). Again the suggestion was made to Bartók of what the piece should be like (a two-movement rhapsody for violin, clarinet and piano lasting six or seven minutes) and again Bartók wrote what he wanted – a rather longer piece, originally in two movements, and performed as such in August 1938, but later expanded it into a three-movement piece of about fifteen minutes' duration. Bartók, Szigeti and Goodman recorded this final version, with its eventual title of *Contrasts*, in New York in 1940.

The *verbunkos* sound is more than ever in evidence in the Violin Concerto and *Contrasts*. It is unmistakable in the opening of the Concerto, with the throbbing harp chords, one of Bartók's favourite sounds, like a bard's accompaniment to the singing rhapsodic line of the violin. The effect of this, in the end, is that Bartók has brought

Horthy with Rudolf Hess
and others inspecting the
site of the 1938 Nazi
Congress at Nuremberg

the Romantic, nationalist concerto of Dvořák and Suk up to date. Székely had been living in the Netherlands since the early 1920s, and this was where the Concerto was first performed, in March 1939 in a Concertgebouw Orchestra concert (under Mengelberg), where it shared the programme with the Egmont overture and Tchaikovsky's Fourth Symphony.

As early as November 1937 Bartók had started to think about sending his manuscripts outside Hungary for safe-keeping, and after the Anschluss he put his plan into action. He divided his work, into juvenilia and sketches (all of which he had retained) and published music, and sent the manuscripts of the last in a number of instalments to Mrs Müller-Widmann in Basle. At the same time, Bartók was pondering whether to leave Hungary – he was considering settling in Turkey, among other places. The fact that his mother was still alive and had come back from Bratislava to Hungary was probably the key factor that prevented him from making the decision to go. His ethnomusicological work at the Academy of Sciences was another: at the end of the 1930s, in between his various trips abroad, he was working ten hours a day on the material housed there, while the publication of the tunes collected by him and by Kodály was still due to go ahead.

Bartók's hesitation over his departure mirrored the uncertainty of the Hungarian government's intentions. There were various National Socialist parties in existence from 1937 onwards, but the leading role was eventually played by the supposedly moderate (but anti-Semitic) right-wing group, the Arrow Cross party. The extreme right-wing had expected to have the Burgenland area of eastern Austria restored to Hungary in the wake of the Anschluss, but in fact no revisions to the country's borders were made until after the Munich Agreement in September 1938, when the southern part of Slovakia was restored in the first 'Vienna Award'. While the Prime Minister Béla Imrédy was negotiating with Britain for its support, Horthy, who had appointed him, was on a state visit to Nazi Germany. Anti-Semitism was well established in a series of laws in Hungary, beginning in 1938. The double game the country was playing did not pay off; too attracted by the promise of restored territory – Ruthenia (now Carpatho-Ukraine) in the north-east, followed in April by eastern Slovakia – Hungary finally had to make a choice, and they chose alliance with Nazi Germany. The country left the League of Nations in the same month.

Members of a right-wing youth movement demonstrating in Budapest in 1938 over the Slovak-Hungarian border dispute. Each placard calls for the return of a former Hungarian possession.

Bartók was aware that 'nearly all our educated Christians are adherents of the Nazi regime', and he wrote, 'I feel quite ashamed of coming from this class'. While Europe waited for war to break out, Bartók not only completed the *Mikrokosmos*, but also wrote two of his most gentle pieces: the Divertimento for string orchestra, and his sad sixth and last String Quartet. The Divertimento was the last of the Sacher commissions, and was written in the conductor's chalet in Saanen, Switzerland, in the first two weeks of August 1939. After finishing it, Bartók went straight on to work on the Quartet, another commission from Székely, for his Hungarian Quartet. Sacher came up to the chalet just before war was declared to alert the composer, and Bartók went straight back to Budapest, where he finished the Quartet in November.

It is impossible to listen to the Quartet without some awareness of Bartók's imminent departure for New York. The work is held together by a recurring motto: the viola announces it sadly at the beginning of the work, it precedes the second and third movements, and becomes the whole material of the fourth and last. An ironic note which had appeared from nowhere at the end of the Fifth Quartet when the four

Horthy meets the newly-
elected Pope Pius XII in 1939

instruments strike up a barrel-organ-like tune is a central part of the
vocabulary of the later quartet: the two middle movements have just
this character – a toy-like march and a *burletta*, or little joke. But the
enigmatic motto wins over in the end, and closes the piece in a mood
of farewell.

In December 1939 Béla and Ditta made a brief recital trip to
Italy. Bartók had also visited the country earlier in the year, and this
fact rather muddies the waters of his unbending insistence on having nothing to do with Fascist regimes. His Rome concert on 12
December included the first performance of five of the Six Bulgarian
Dances. He had only just arrived back in Budapest a week later when
his mother died; he was so distressed that he could not even manage
to go to her funeral. Gradually he began to recover a little, but he
confessed that he 'drowned himself in work' to be able to cope.
Months later he was berating himself for all the time he had recently
spent away from his mother – the few weeks in Saanen while he was
composing the Divertimento, for instance. These are hardly unusual
expressions of grief and regret, but there is a childlike quality to
Bartók's grief which is striking in a man of fifty-nine.

*Opposite, Horthy
taking part in a parade in
Budapest in 1940*

Slowly he realized that, with his mother dead, there was now nothing to tie him and his family to Europe, and he and Ditta at last started to make definite plans to leave. It had surely occurred to him that the USA was the safest place to aim for, and that he could make some sort of living there. New York was to be their destination and the composer's last home.

7

Bartók in the garden of the
Csalán út house, 1940

I set out from my lovely home,
my beautiful Hungary.
I looked back halfway along the road,
and my eyes brimmed with tears.

Hungarian folk-song:
'Elindultam szép hazámbul'

Two Pale Emigrants 1939-45

Bartók was ill with flu over Christmas 1939 and again in the spring, and as a result the concert-tour that he and Ditta had planned to make to the USA was postponed until April. By the summer the first signs of his leukaemia were showing themselves, when he began to complain of a pain in his right shoulder, but the disease was not diagnosed until four years later.

Alone, Bartók set sail from Naples on 3 April for the seven-week tour, during which he would try to set up the conditions to allow him and Ditta to move there for the duration of the war. The first concert was a recital with his old friend Szigeti in the Library of Congress in Washington, as part of the Elizabeth Sprague Coolidge Festival. Szigeti had left Hungary to settle in America the previous year, and in his last Budapest recital had played an old Bartók work, the solo violin portrait of Stefi, a young girl from a vanished age in a vanished Hungary.

The Washington concert had a typically balanced programme: Beethoven's 'Kreutzer' Sonata, the Debussy Violin Sonata, and Bartók's own First Rhapsody and Second Violin Sonata. In New York there was a Carnegie Hall concert, with Szigeti clearly the chief attraction ('Only New York Recital This Season'), and the following day, a lecture at Harvard on 'Problems of Folk Music Research in East Europe'. It was in the aftermath of this lecture that Bartók was offered the prospect of congenial work as a research fellow at Columbia University in New York, transcribing a collection of Serbo-Croatian folk recordings which was housed there. There were other offers of work, including a post as a teacher of composition at the Curtis Institute in Philadelphia, which he declined, and given that he had an agent in New York, Andrew Schulhof, the prospects were reasonably good for the Bartóks to move to New York. Bartók, Szigeti and Benny Goodman got together for two days at the end of April to record the complete three-movement *Contrasts* for Columbia Records in New York.

Bartók's only involvement in this Carnegie Hall recital in 1940 was to accompany Szigeti in the First Rhapsody for violin and piano.

Bartók returned to Europe in the middle of May, and began preparations for the return trip. The Divertimento had its first performance in Basle, given by Sacher's orchestra, but Bartók did not attend. He and his wife were reported in the Hungarian press to be planning a three-month concert tour abroad, and it is possible that Bartók was still, at this late stage, undecided about how long he would stay away. According to his son Béla, it was never his intention to emigrate on a permanent basis. He had taken three Polish refugees into the house in Csalán út, and in October asked his elder son to take responsibility for the property (Péter was away at boarding school). The furniture was left behind, but all other materials went with Bartók to America; most of the manuscripts were long gone, first to

Szigeti, Bartók and
Goodman recording
Contrasts in the Columbia
recording studio, New York,
April 1940

Switzerland and London, then on to New York. In making his will
Bartók took the opportunity to express his disgust at what had
happened to his country:

> *As long as the former Oktogon-tér and Körönd bear the names of the*
> *two men after whom they are now named, and further, as long as there*
> *shall be any squares or streets in Hungary named after these two men,*
> *no square, street or public building shall be named after me in this*
> *country; and until then no memorial plaque for me shall be put in any*
> *public place.*

The two locations Bartók was referring to are junctions on one of
Pest's principal boulevards, on which the Opera House stands. Bartók
did not live to see those two names (Hitler and Mussolini) replaced
briefly after the war by those of Stalin and Lenin.

The Bartóks gave a farewell concert in the hall of the Music
Academy on 8 October: this was the occasion of Ditta's debut as
a soloist, playing Mozart's F major concerto, No. 11, K. 413 (387a).
The only item for both of them was the Mozart two-piano concerto
in E flat, K. 365 (316a). Bartók finished the programme with some
items from *Mikrokosmos*. Four days later they set off by train, via
Milan, for Geneva. The visa arrangements for a journey like this were
daunting: visas to enter the USA, and three separate ones to cross
Italy, France and Spain. Bartók's Zurich-based European agent, Walter
Schulthess (who had married Stefi Geyer), presumably was responsible
for the travel arrangements. Stefi came to Geneva to see the couple
off, and the sadness of this farewell and the reminiscences it called up

The first edition of
Mikrokosmos, Bartók's
collection of 153 educational
piano pieces of progressive
difficulty, 1940

153 PROGRESSIVE PIANO PIECES

IN SIX VOLUMES

BOOSEY & HAWKES I~N~C.

can only be imagined. On the morning of the 15th the Bartóks went by coach all the way to Barcelona; from there they took a train to Lisbon, where they boarded SS *Escalibur* for New York. Their luggage was held up at the border between France and Spain, and was not seen again until the following February, when Bartók went to the docks in Jersey City to collect it. The missing trunks must have caused profound distress when the couple was trying to settle in their new home: not only were there replaceable items inside (Ditta's shoes and clothes, and bits and pieces of their concert outfits), but the accumulated possessions of a lifetime (Bartók never threw anything away), with all their associations of home, and most importantly, some of Bartók's folk-song manuscripts.

Bartók's years in exile in the USA have been seen in conflicting ways. There are those who, like Stravinsky, see his decline and 'death in circumstances of actual need … as one of the tragedies of our society'. Others claim that Bartók was fairly well provided for, able to earn a reasonable living until the advance of his leukaemia, when the American Society for Composers, Authors and Publishers undertook to pay his medical expenses. Some portray him as isolated and unhappy in the urban jungle, others as belonging to two small networks of Hungarian exiles, and sympathetic musicians. Some emigrés belonged to both categories, like the conductor Fritz Reiner or the pianist György Sándor. He was in touch with former pupils, and had a Hungarian doctor and solicitor.

Bartók with conductor Rudolf Kolisch during a rehearsal for a performance of *Music for Strings, Percussion and Celesta* given at the New School of Social Research, New York, 11 December 1940

Things did look promising at first; Columbia awarded him an honorary doctorate in November 1940 (Bartók gives an amusing description of the ceremony, to the muted background of discreet organ music), and his work as a research fellow could hardly have been better suited. A Harvard professor, Milman Parry, had made about 2,600 recordings of folk material in Yugoslavia in the mid-1930s, many of them of the epic ballads which most interested him. It was Parry's idea that the performance of these, to the accompaniment of the single-string gusle, related them to the poetry of antiquity, but Bartók was aware that there were analogies from further afield, and there are similar styles of performance to be found as far away as Mongolia. Parry had died suddenly in 1935, and Bartók was to join the American's former collaborator, Albert Lord, in the work of transcription. However, Bartók proposed to transcribe not only

Béla and Ditta take their seats for a two-piano recital in the Town Hall, New York, 24 November 1940. The programme included seven pieces from *Mikrokosmos* arranged for two pianos and Debussy's *En blanc et noir*.

the epics, but the other songs which had been recorded, and which possibly interested him more. He suggested to the University administration that while the transcribed epics could be of interest for study at Harvard, the accompanying collection of 'women's songs' – which were similar to the material he was used to working on – could be published.

Before starting work for Columbia in premises owned by the university in 117th Street in March 1941, he and Ditta gave a number of concerts – one in New York shortly after arriving, followed by a tour at the beginning of the year, taking them as far as San Francisco and Seattle. Bartók named Detroit as the city where they had the best reception. They also got some impression of the Eastern European presence in America: the janitor of his first, Long Island apartment block was a Slovakian from Kosice who spoke both Slovakian and Hungarian, and in Cleveland Bartók attended a celebration with gypsy music in the Hungarian community ('Hungarians here, there and everywhere; but we cannot be happy about this because the second generation already speaks the language brokenly').

The Columbia appointment was due to run until June 1942, and Bartók was in correspondence throughout the year with the University

of Washington in Seattle, making arrangements for a post which he could take up after that time. Seattle had a collection of recordings of North American Indian music, which Bartók proposed to transcribe, and in addition he would lecture on the study of folk music. Columbia extended Bartók's contract until December 1942, and the likely starting-date of the Seattle appointment was postponed.

Bartók's sixtieth birthday passed without any public recognition in the USA: he wrote to his son that apart from five telegrams of greetings, there was no interest in his birthday. In Budapest, in contrast, one of the last issues of *Nyugat*, dated 1 April, celebrated the event, with a piece by the musicologist Bence Szabolcsi outlining the stages in Bartók's musical development.

The political mood Bartók encountered in the USA in 1941 was split between those who wanted to intervene in the European war, and those who wanted nothing to do with it. Bartók had a conversation with a former US Ambassador to Hungary, who, he wrote, spoke sympathetically about the country, and there was no question of where the White House's sympathies lay. Roosevelt, in the first year of his third term as president, put his Lend-Lease programme of arming the Allies into operation, and had secret meetings with Churchill. When a German U-Boat fired on a US destroyer in September, it gave him the opportunity to order any Axis boat within the American Defense Zone to be shot at, and at the end of the year the Japanese attack on Pearl Harbor in Hawaii brought the USA into a war that was now genuinely global. Hungary entered the war in June on the Axis side, when it joined 'Operation Barbarossa' against the Soviet Union, and Britain responded by declaring war on Hungary. But by November the advance on Russia was stalled, and huge numbers of Hungarian troops were lost.

In 1942, with the country now mobilized for war, the University of Washington in Seattle began to prevaricate; it was not known if there would be funds for Bartók's appointment. Opportunities for giving concerts were declining too. Ralph Hawkes, who was trying to promote the Bartóks and the composer's works published by Boosey and Hawkes found concert organizers unwilling to engage the couple, and performers just as unwilling to play Bartók's music. Bartók had seemingly lost whatever slim hold he had once had on American audiences; his music would have been perceived as too

'difficult' for a nation at war. While it was hardly obligatory for every performer to be a glamorous figure, it is true that these were not thin on the ground, and Bartók would have paled into the background behind the likes of Stokowski, Rachmaninov or Horowitz. A little sidelight is thrown on Bartók's relations with Boosey and Hawkes by a letter to him from Hans Heinsheimer, who had followed the composer from UE to Boosey's, and was involved in organizing concerts for him. He complains to the composer about his nit-picking criticisms, and his failure ever to show gratitude for what the company was doing on his behalf. Bartók's reply is not known. But for Boosey and Hawkes Bartók was to be an important and lucrative acquisition, and elsewhere Heinsheimer writes of the privilege of his association with him.

The Bartóks' first apartment was in Forest Hills on Long Island. A piano company helpfully provided two instruments, but there was no room large enough to hold both of them, and the couple were obliged to practise their two-piano repertoire in adjoining rooms.

Bartók on the veranda of Agatha Fassett's house in Riverton, NY, summer 1941. Agatha Fassett was one of several Hungarian-Americans with whom the Bartóks mixed in the USA.

BARTÓK
plays
BARTÓK
SONATA FOR TWO PIANOS AND PERCUSSION

BÉLA & DITTA PASZTORY BARTÓK

pianists

Harry J. Baker & Edward J. Rubsan

percussionists

10 Pieces from FOR CHILDREN

EVENING IN
TRANSYLVANIA &
BEAR'S DANCE
from 10 EASY PIECES

Béla Bartók, Piano
Title Announcements in Hungarian
by Bartók

Bartók made a number of
official recordings released
by CBS in the USA, as well
as these performances
recorded for CBS Radio and
later issued commercially.

An old complaint of Bartók's naturally surfaced again: the building
was too close to a main road, and the noise made it impossible for
him to work in peace. By May 1941 they had moved from Forest Hills
into an apartment in Riverdale, in the Bronx. This was a district
rather similar to the area round Csalán út, suburban, leafy and quiet,
and the home of a number of musicians, including Toscanini. They
were helped in their house-hunting by Agatha Fassett (the married
name of Ágota Illés), who had in earlier years taken music lessons at
the Academy in Budapest. Béla and Ditta, and Péter when he reached

America, all stayed at her holiday home in the Vermont countryside in the first years of their time in the USA, and she later wrote an elaborate recollection of her friendship with the Bartóks in a colourful book, *The Naked Face of Genius*. Many aspects of Bartók's character surface in her reporting of his conversations: a Puritanism where material things are concerned, a lack of social graces and absorption in his own concerns to the point of rudeness, and even a certain timidity faced with the demands of life in New York.

These are personal memories, of course, but many are backed up in the recollections of others who had dealings with him during these difficult years. Some more objective anecdotes show how Bartók's attachment to nature manifested itself: the story of how he smelled horses on the dark streets of New York, near Central Park (and sure enough, there was a riding stable nearby), and the scene he made over bread dough being stirred in a porcelain bowl with a metal spoon in the middle of the afternoon. According to him, bread should only be made at dawn, in a wooden trough, and kneaded by women's hands. Readers today might wonder why he didn't offer to bake the bread himself. Others have testified to his concern for all living creatures: he would not allow the chickens that the family kept during World War I to be killed for food, and when indulging his interest in collecting insects, he would smother them so that they would not feel pain.

Agatha Fassett's rambling story of Bartók's empathy with a family cat fits into this pattern. The portrait of Ditta that she gives is of an unpredictable, if not imbalanced woman, and whatever tensions may have existed in the couple's relationship before, they are bound to have been exacerbated by the difficulties of their new life, and Bartók's gradually worsening health. It is also interesting that Bartók, who was normally so scathing about the musical tastes of middle-class Hungary, should have himself become a sort of 'light classic' for the educated Hungarians he encountered in America, as is borne out by their requests for him to play his old piano stand-bys *Allegro barbaro*, 'Bear Dance' and 'Evening with the Székelys'.

Péter Bartók arrived in New York unannounced in April 1942. He had left Budapest the previous Christmas, and although his parents knew that he had set sail from Lisbon, they did not know which boat he was on; his father met him by chance at the subway station near their home. Péter went on to join the US Navy and to fight in the

war, and remained in the USA even when his mother returned to Budapest in 1946.

The decline in Bartók's health began at this time. He had high temperatures and a persistent stiffness in his right shoulder, but nothing was diagnosed, and no treatment given.

There was no new music written during these first two years in America; Bartók was involved only with making arrangements of two older pieces, specifically as repertoire for himself and Ditta. The first was a transcription of the Sonata for Two Pianos and Percussion, which changed it into a concerto for two pianos, percussion and orchestra. This was finished in December 1940, but the first perform-ance was not given in the USA, or by the Bartóks. The première was in London, in November 1942, and the Bartóks' own performance followed in January 1943, with Fritz Reiner conducting the New York Philharmonic. Bartók never played in public again.

A more surprising choice of work to transcribe was the Second Orchestral Suite of 1905–7. Bartók arranged this as a Suite for Two Pianos in 1941, and gave the four movements descriptive titles: *Serenata*, *Allegro diabolico*, *Scena della puszta*, and *Per finire*. He and Ditta toured with the piece early in 1942 (the première was in Chicago in January), part of a programme which included some of Colin McPhee's transcriptions of Balinese gamelan music. Later, in the light of the transcription of the suite, he made some further revisions to the orchestral original.

After his last public concert Bartók's life became a battle against ill-health, and it stayed that way, with numerous lulls and temporary victories, until his death two-and-a-half years later. When his post at Columbia was not renewed, Harvard contacted him to give a series of lectures, to start in February 1943. He prepared four papers, which he read during that month. Four years earlier Stravinsky, who had only just arrived in the USA, read his 'Poetics of Music' addresses to the same university. Bartók's lectures are far less pretentious and dog-matic, although in Stravinsky's defence it should be said that he was filling a chair of poetry, not of music (and did not in fact write the texts of his lectures). While Bartók digresses to cover other artistic concerns in a somewhat superficial way, his subject is definitely music: folk, that of other composers, and his own. Much of what he has to say is genuinely revealing of his approach to composition, and has

perhaps been overlooked by later analysts who have tried to find
Lendvai's theories proved in every last detail, to the point of absurdity.
The central point reinforced by what he has to say is that Bartók
arrived at his method 'subconsciously and instinctively'.

*This attitude does not mean that I composed without ... set plans and
without sufficient control. The plans were concerned with the spirit of the
new work and the technical problems ... all more or less instinctively felt,
but I never was concerned with general theories to be applied to the works
I was about to write. Now that the greatest part of my work has already
been written, certain general tendencies appear – general formulas from
which theories can be deduced. But even now I would prefer to try new
ways and means instead of deducing theories.*

Immediately after the lectures he collapsed and was rushed to
Mount Sinai hospital, where tuberculosis was diagnosed. Bartók was
not a member of the American Society for Composers, Authors and
Publishers, but on the insistence of his former pupil Ernő Balogh,
who had settled in the USA, ASCAP sent two representatives of their
welfare division to the hospital. Subsequently the society took over
the financial responsibility for all Bartók's medical treatment; he was
transferred to a different hospital, where a different diagnosis was
made. Péter Bartók wrote to his half-brother after their father's death,
that although the doctors 'knew – or at least thought – that it was
a leukaemia, they told us that it was a polycythemia'. So Bartók and
his family were kept in the dark about the nature of his illness, and
continued to expect that there would be a return to health, when this
was not now realistic.

In the summer Serge Koussevitzky, principal conductor of the
Boston Symphony Orchestra, and not someone particularly noted
for promoting Bartók's work, visited the composer in hospital with
a commission for a piece for his orchestra. In fact, the idea for the
commission had come from Fritz Reiner and Szigeti, and it was they
who had prompted Koussevitzky's visit. The fee of $1,000 was pro-
vided by the Koussevitzky Foundation (in memory of the conductor's
late wife), in the customary arrangement of one half on acceptance
and the balance on submission of the score. It seems that Bartók was
still capable of bristling at any suggestion that he was being helped

financially, and a lot of pressure was brought to bear on him to
persuade him to take the advance.

Bartók then set off with Ditta to a summer retreat at Saranac Lake
in the Adirondacks, near to a tuberculosis sanatorium. In mid-August
he got down to writing the Concerto for Orchestra, which he worked
on incessantly and had finished by the time he got back to New York
in October. The title suggests that he still had no intention of writing
a symphony (although Bartók's own programme note for the work
describes it as 'symphony-like'); indeed he felt that the symphony was
dead. Bartók's straightforward explanation of the title is the piece's
'tendency to treat the single instruments or instrument groups in
a 'concertant' or soloistic manner'. It was not an original concept –
Hindemith wrote his Concerto for Orchestra in 1925, and Kodály his
in 1939 – but it certainly proved to be the perfect context for Bartók
to display his individual strengths as a creator of orchestral sounds.

If Bartók thought that the symphony was dead it is understandable
why he chose to send up a theme from Shostakovitch's 'Leningrad'
Symphony in the fourth movement of the Concerto. What is perhaps
surprising is that Bartók gave the work a programmatic content:
'a gradual transition from the sternness of the first movement and the

The 22-year-old Yehudi
Menuhin, 1938. Menuhin
played two Bartók works
(the Second Violin Concerto
and Second Violin Sonata)
for the first time in 1943.
In the same period he met
the composer and commis-
sioned the Solo Violin Sonata.

Bartók with his piano pupil Ann Chenee in his flat on 57th Street, New York, 1943. On the piano are copies of *Mikrokosmos* and *For Children*; the portraits on the wall are of Brahms, Liszt, Schumann and Busoni.

lugubrious death-song of the third, to the life-assertion of the last one'. This sounds suspiciously like the programme of a symphonic poem by Richard Strauss: if the concerto is a kind of summation of a lifetime of composing, then there may indeed by a place in it for a recollection of the very beginnings of Bartók's orchestral work.

The piece has the five movements of the familiar Bartók palindrome: a central slow movement is framed by two Scherzos and two outer movements each in a kind of sonata form. There is little that is new about the content; the value of the work lies in its assurance, the sense of Bartók finding the right place for everything. Even the humour is gentler than before, and the jocular title of the first Scherzo, 'Giuoco delle coppie', was intended to be a bland 'Presentation of the pairs', not 'game of'. The second, an 'Intermezzo interrotto' (echoes of Debussy) may mock the 'Leningrad' Symphony, but it does so only to underline the pathos and nostalgia of a semi-

quoted Hungarian song, 'Szép vagy, gyönyörű vagy, Magyarország' ('Hungary you are beautiful, you are lovely'), from Zsigmond Vincze's 1928 operetta *The Bride of Hamburg*.

It has often been noticed that the 'Leningrad' motif is reminiscent of a tune in *The Merry Widow* (and Shostakovitch may have chosen it himself in ironic portrayal of the Nazis, since the operetta was popularly said to be a favourite of Hitler's); when this was suggested to Bartók he claimed not to know the Léhar. It is really only in these two movements that the instruments are used in a concertante manner. Elsewhere, as Bartók himself pointed out, it is the idea of instrumental virtuosity that prevails: the brass piling in on each other in the first movement or the strings scrubbing relentlessly at the beginning of the last.

The work is the quintessential orchestral showpiece, the ideal work for this particular time in the musical life of the USA, when the great American orchestras were under the music directorships of more-or-less recent emigrés from Europe – Toscanini, Stokowski, Mitropoulos,

Front cover and inside of the programme for the first New York performance of the Concerto for Orchestra, 10 January 1944. The piece had already been given four times in Boston the previous month, and enthusiastically received.

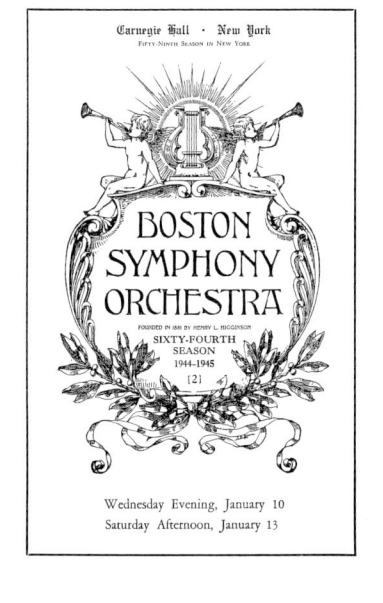

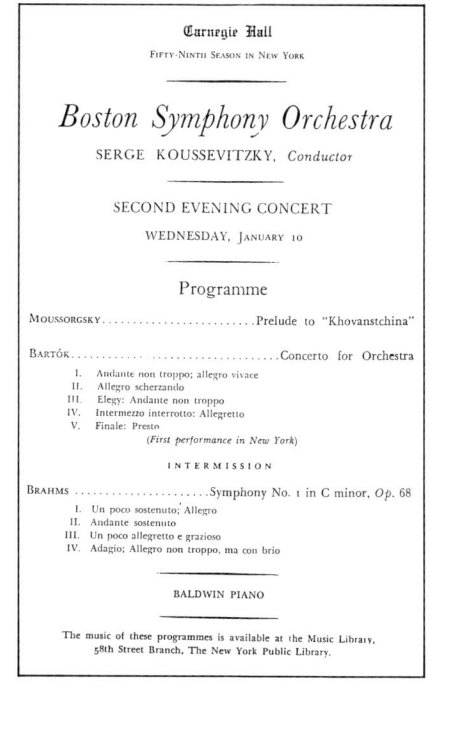

Ormandy, Walter. This was that delicate moment when, as the cliché has it, the efficiency and skill of the orchestral players encountered the inherited traditions of European music-making, and produced some remarkable results.

Back in New York Bartók heard for the first time a performance of his 1938 Violin Concerto, played by Tossy Spivakovsky at Carnegie Hall. The violinist Yehudi Menuhin had contacted Bartók from his home in California the year before, enquiring about performing the Violin Concerto, By this time he had added the piece to his repertoire, and played it in Minneapolis under Mitropoulos. When Menuhin came to New York in December 1943 he played through the First Violin Sonata with Bartók. The meeting started coolly, with no display of charm or polite words of welcome from Bartók, but he was enormously impressed by the violinist's playing, and said so, albeit in his typically uneffusive, way. Menuhin offered to commission a short violin work, and the result was the Bach-like Sonata for solo violin, which Bartók finished the following March.

When the Bartóks came back from that first trip to Saranac Lake it was to a new home, or homes. They left the Riverdale house and Bartók rented a small apartment on 57th Street just below Central Park (and along from Carnegie Hall) for Ditta and Péter, and took a room for himself in a hotel, not far away. There seems to be no logical explanation for this arrangement, and there is no other evidence of a breakdown in his relationship with Ditta. All the accommodation was paid for by ASCAP. In December he left for Asheville, North Carolina, on an ASCAP-funded convalescent trip, where he wrote the piece for Menuhin, and worked on the Serbo-Croatian songs. His Columbia post had been renewed for a further six months, starting in April, at the instigation of his lawyer, Viktor Bátor, but Bartók was not strong enough to take it up.

When Bartók came back from Asheville in April to the Woodrow Hotel he had a relapse: this is when his doctor Israel Rappaport, a fellow Hungarian emigré, first diagnosed leukaemia. The summer was again spent at Saranac Lake. Here Bartók tinkered with details of the Violin Sonata in response to Menuhin's fingering and bowing marks. The piece was performed in New York in November, a week before the first triumphant performances of the Concerto for Orchestra. These took place in December in Boston, with the same

Romanian troops engaged
in street-fighting after
reaching Budapest late in
1944. Romania, originally
allied to Nazi Germany,
signed an armistice with the
Soviet Union in 1944 and
took part in the Red Army's
advance on Hungary.

Two Pale Emigrants 1939-45

programme (Mozart's *Idomeneo* overture and the Franck Symphony) being played twice, at a Friday matineé and a Saturday evening concert. With less than a year left to live Bartók was turning into a popular composer. Koussevitzky's opinion of the concerto became more and more enthusiastic: 'the best orchestra piece of the last twenty-five years' is how Bartók reported it, and two more performances were given in Boston at the end of the month.

Yet another commission turned up, this time for a concerto for the viola player William Primrose. In January 1945 Primrose visited the composer in the 57th Street apartment which Béla and Ditta were now sharing (presumably because Péter was now away from home, having enlisted in the navy). He was due to play the Walton Viola Concerto and Bartók was planning to attend the concert, but in the end he was too ill, and listened to the broadcast. He started drafting a piece, but his attention at this stage was more directed towards a work he was writing in secret for Ditta's forty-second birthday on 31 October – a third piano concerto. In the end he finished neither work entirely. The Piano Concerto was completed in short score, and orchestrated up to the last seventeen bars. His Hungarian colleague Tibor Serly visited him in September 1945 on the evening before Bartók went into hospital for the last time, and interrupted him working on the end of the Piano Concerto. Feeling that it was his visit which had prevented Bartók from finishing the piece, he considered it his duty to orchestrate the last bars.

The score was prepared for publication by Bartók's long-standing editor Erwin Stein. His painstaking preparation of the published score uses different sizes of type to distinguish Bartók's own markings from those of the editors. The Viola Concerto remained a draft (there were only thirteen pages of sketches to go on) but Serly assembled a work from this material. This posthumous piece with its sometimes crude orchestration, thin, naïve motifs, and patent errors of judgement is increasingly being called into question (although violists have been glad of its existence). A new edition prepared by Péter Bartók and Nelson Dellamaggiore, who have gone back to the original material, is to be published in 1995.

The last Piano Concerto is by far the gentlest of the three, and the simplest to play. It is solidly in Bartók's last manner, a sort of mellowed Baroque, and has many of the composer's familiar touches,

although the music of the night is replaced by a flurry of bird song:
Bartók had been noting down bird calls in Asheville. There is
a chorale, marked, uniquely for Bartók, Adagio religioso, and a finale
that intersperses a folk-dance theme with running Bach-like motifs.
While he was writing his Concerto, Bartók got to know for the first
time that staple of the Romantic piano repertoire, Grieg's Piano
Concerto. The first performance had to wait until February 1946,
when Bartók's former pupil, György Sándor played it with the
Philadelphia Orchestra under Eugene Ormandy.

Reports were finally coming through from Hungary, and Bartók
was catching up on the news from a Hungarian-language newspaper,
Szabadság ('Liberty'), published in Cleveland. The German army
invaded Hungary in March 1944, and any opponents of National
Socialism were deported to concentration camps, and Jews outside
Budapest were sent to their deaths. This was nothing, however,
compared to the events later in the year, and over the winter months
into early 1945. In August Horthy was hoping to switch sides (as
Romania had already done); the tightening advance of the Allies after
D-Day would have convinced him that this was the only way to
survive. When the Red Army entered Hungary the following month
he arranged for an armistice with the Soviet Union.

The Germans reacted by taking over in Hungary, with the aid of
the home-grown Fascists, the Arrow Cross, and terror ensued. Most
of Budapest's Jews were deported to death camps (although more
escaped death than in other central European cities). The capital itself
was ravaged by fighting during the winter, and when the Red Army
occupied it in February all the bridges across the Danube were down.
By April the entire country was under the military occupation of the
Red Army. With word of these events trickling through, it must have
been an enormous relief for Bartók to hear that his son Béla was safe,
as were Elza and the Kodálys. In the summer of 1945, it cannot have
seemed feasible or practical to return to a ruined city in a country
under army occupation. So the Bartóks chose not to go back for the
time being.

Following page, makeshift Béla and Ditta once again spent the summer at Saranac Lake,
wooden crosses are erected but this time he was determined to pay for himself, so their accom-
in a bombed cemetery in modation was less grand than before. The spot was also convenient
Budapest, 1944 for Bartók to go through the rigmarole of obtaining US citizenship:

> **BARTOK—Bela,** on Wednesday, Sept. 26, beloved husband of Edith Bartok, father of Bela and Peter Bartok. Services at "The Universal Chapel." Lexington Ave., at 52d St., on Friday, Sept. 28, at 2 P. M.
>
> **BARTOK—Bela.** We announce with profound sorrow the death of the distinguished composer, Bela Bartok, in New York on Sept. 26, 1945.
>
> DEEMS TAYLOR, President. American Society of Composers, Authors and Publishers.

The announcement of Bartók's death in the New York Times, 27 September 1945

he travelled to Montreal at the beginning of July to be able to re-enter the USA. Péter, who had been stationed in Panama, was now demobilized and joined his parents at the lake. Bartók was even well enough to do some climbing with his son, but he collapsed at the end of August, and the family went back to New York.

According to Ditta, Bartók was depressed to be back in the apartment. He did occupy himself with work, however, writing on 8 September to Serly that the draft of the Viola Concerto was ready, and promising an orchestral score in five or six weeks' time. But on the 22nd he was taken into the West Side Hospital, and four days later, with Ditta and Péter on either side of his bed, each holding one hand, he died.

The funeral service took place on the 28th, in a Unitarian chapel on Lexington Avenue, and the burial was in a rather superior cemetery, Ferncliff in Hartsdale, New York. Thinking ahead to the eventual possibility of the remains being taken back to Hungary, ASCAP ensured that there was an outer coffin of bronze. Bartók's remains were finally returned to Hungary in 1988. In the meantime the Cold War placed a barrier between his two countries; propaganda battles were fought, and the manuscripts were divided between Budapest and New York. Complementary archives existed in both cities, and although detailed plans have been made for a complete critical edition of

Bartók's works, total agreement has not yet (1995) been reached to allow this to go ahead.

Ditta found the first year without her husband extremely hard; her health declined, and eventually she went into hospital. She and Péter made a last trip to Saranac Lake in the summer of 1946, and it was then that she decided to go back to Budapest. It was only in the 1960s that she began to play in public again, performing for the first time the Piano Concerto that her husband had left for her. She died in 1982.

Very soon after Bartók's death, many of his mature works became popular modern classics. The American pieces, especially, were in the forefront, but the works from the 1930s were not far behind. At the beginning I wrote about the Hungarian-ness of Bartók's music; it is just as important to stress how Eastern Europe as a whole resonates in his work. His influence on younger composers after his death was mostly heard in Eastern Europe, not just because of the political importance of folk music in the countries of the Warsaw Pact, or because the West was wrapped up in its alternative, serial orthodoxy, but because the sound and aesthetic of Bartók's music springs from a shared culture.

If there are jokes in Haydn's symphonies (players tuning-up or stealing away, and other such 'surprises'), there are at least as many in Bartók's works: the barrel-organ in the Fifth Quartet, the chain

Bartók's remains were returned to Hungary in 1988 and re-buried in this tomb in Budapest.

of comical references in the 'Intermezzo interrotto', even the kitsch
cadence at the end of the Sonata for Two Pianos and Percussion.
There is a cultural unity in the region that links Bartók with some
of his contemporaries: the quirky Janáček, with one foot in the nineteenth century and the other in a private world of natural sound;
Martinů, as well, for all his stylistic instability, strayed directly into
Bartók territory (with the Concerto for Two Pianos, for instance).
But these were not universally-acclaimed figures at the time: their
significance and their connections with Bartók were only revealed as
time froze over to become history. Van Dieren and Sibelius were
the big names of the 1920s and 1930s in northern Europe and northern America. Van Dieren has stayed trapped under the ice, and
Bartók was ready to bet that the same would happen to Sibelius.

In the post-war world it was still in Eastern Europe that the spirit
of Bartók was best evoked, in the work of the Polish composers who
leapt to fame in the 1950s. The surface sound of Lutosławski's 1956
Musique Funèbre for strings, dedicated to Bartók's memory, suggests
that the influence has not been digested, although the technique used
is Lutosławski's own. By the time of the masterly *Livre pour orchestre*
(1967) the composer is totally sure of himself. The structure still has
something of Bartók, however, evoking the Sixth Quartet: four movements with a 'motto' in between (in this case orchestral doodling,
to suggest skimming between the chapters of the 'book') which eventually becomes the material for the last movement.

Bartók is not really in the mainstream of ethnomusicological
practice either; his role is more as a precursor than a founding father
of the wider discipline which developed after 1945, like all those who
were primarily concerned with collecting, codifying and preserving
folk material.

For all that he provides a direct link to Liszt in his piano-playing,
he does not really belong in the hall of fame with other great pianists
of the twentieth century. There is something oddly apologetic about
his recorded performances, and however intriguing and charming, the
introspection of his playing is a little short on intensity. But a composer is not necessarily the best advocate of his own music: the work
may still be open each time he chooses to play it, and there may be
aspects of the music which the composer can hear, but does not bring
out for the listener. And for all Bartók's insistence on exactitude, there

is a noticeable gap between his written directions, and especially the meticulous timings provided in the published scores (the duration of each section within each movement), and the free, creative performances preserved on record.

Bartók also stands to one side of the idea of 'folk-based' composition. In the same way that the sources trawled by Stravinsky to create his neo-classicism range much more widely than is suggested by the simple phrase 'back-to-Bach', so Bartók's technique is much more than the transplantation of folk material into art music. Other composers, before and after Bartók, better represent this concept, with its attendant nationalist features, in many of their works: Vaughan Williams in England, Copland in the USA, and, it must be said, Kodály in Hungary.

Overwhelmingly, Bartók's contribution to music is as the composer of a huge number of works in the standard repertoire. More than any of his contemporaries, he gave a wide range of musicians – pianists, violinists, orchestras and string quartets – pieces of music to play that are indisputably twentieth-century classics. Although he often wrote works in pairs, the second attempt was never a copy of the first, and there was always a surprise in store as each work came into being. It is impossible to imagine the Seventh Quartet that was in the composer's mind when he died, or the unwritten cantatas that were to have accompanied *Cantata profana*. Equally it is hard to imagine the twentieth century without the work which Bartók did complete, progressive in content, but set within conventional formats, experimental in sound, but constructed with care and precision. The single most striking aspect of the music is its humanity, and whatever awkward face Bartók may have presented to the world, this quality is what endures.

Classified List of Works

Bartók started listing his works at opus 1 in 1890, went as far as opus 31, and then began again at opus 1 in 1894 with a piano sonata. This second listing was abandoned, and it was only with his 1904 Rhapsody for piano and orchestra that he began to give opus numbers to his mature work. This continued until the First Sonata for violin and piano of 1921 (whose number was later removed), but arrangements of folk material such as *For Children* were excluded. Denijs Dille catalogued Bartók's works of 1890–1904 in *Thematisches Verzeichnis der Jugendwerke Béla Bartóks* (1974). These are indicated below by DD. The mature works are known by their Sz number, according to the standard catalogue by András Szőllősy which appears in *Bartók: sa vie et son oeuvre* (1956), and which was revised in Ujfalussy's *Béla Bartók* (1965). Arrangements of works not made by Bartók himself have been excluded. I am indebted to Malcolm Gillies's revision of the work list in Halsey Stevens's *Life and Music of Béla Bartók* for information concerning first performances (given after 'fp' below); works whose performance details are not known are marked 'fp?'.

Stage Works

Duke Bluebeard's Castle (A Kékszakállú herceg vára), Op. 11, Sz 48, opera in one act, for soloists and orchestra, libretto by Béla Balázs (1911, revised 1912, 1918). fp Budapest, 24 May 1918

The Wooden Prince (A fából faragott királyfi), Op. 13, Sz 60, ballet in one act, libretto by Béla Balázs (1914–17). fp Budapest, 12 May 1917

The Miraculous Mandarin (A csodálatos mandarin), Op. 19, Sz 73, pantomime in one act, libretto by Menyhért Lengyel (1918-19, orchestrated 1923, revised 1924, 1926–31). fp Cologne, 27 November 1926

Orchestral

Valcer, DD 60b (*c.* 1900). fp?

Scherzo, DD 65 (*c.* 1901). fp?

Symphony, DD 68 (1902, orchestrated 1903). fp Scherzo only, Budapest, 29 February 1904

Kossuth, symphonic poem, DD 75a (1903). fp Budapest,13 January 1904

Rhapsody, for piano and orchestra, Op. 1, Sz 27, arrangement of Sz 26 (1904?). fp Paris, August 1905

Scherzo, for piano and orchestra, Op. 2, Sz 28, alsoentitled Burlesque (1904). fp Budapest, 28 September 1961

Suite No. 1, Op. 3, Sz 31 (1905, revised c. 1920). fpp Movements 1–3 only, Vienna, 19 November 1905; complete, Budapest, 1 March 1909

Suite No. 2, Op. 4, Sz 34 (1905, 1907, revised 1920, 1943). fpp Movement 2 only, Berlin, 2 January 1909; complete, Budapest, 22 November 1909

Violin Concerto ('No. 1'), Sz 36 (1907–8). fp Basle, 30 May 1958

Two Portraits (Két portré), Op. 5, Sz 37 (No. 1 1907–8, No. 2 orchestrated 1911). fpp No. 1, Budapest, 12 February 1911; complete, Budapest, 20 April 1916

Two Pictures (Két kép), Op. 10, Sz 46 (1910). fp Budapest, 25 February 1913

Romanian Dance (Román tánc), Sz 47a (1911). fp 12 February 1911

Four Pieces, Op. 12, Sz 51 (1912, orchestrated 1921). fp Budapest, 9 January 1922

The Wooden Prince, suite, Op. 13, Sz 60 (1921–4?). fp Budapest, 23 November 1931

Romanian Folkdances (Román népi táncok), Sz 68, arrangement of piano pieces (1917). fp Budapest, 11 February 1918

The Miraculous Mandarin, suite, Op. 19, Sz 73 (1919, 1927). fp Budapest, 15 October 1928

Dance Suite (Táncsvit, originally Tánc-Suite), Sz 77 (1923). fp Budapest, 19 November 1923

Piano Concerto No. 1, Sz 83 (1926). fp Frankfurt am Main, 1 July 1927

Rhapsody No. 1, for violin and orchestra, Sz 87 (1928). fp Königsberg, 1 November 1929

Rhapsody No. 2, for violin and orchestra, Sz 90 (1928, revised 1944). fp Budapest, 26 November 1929

Piano Concerto No. 2, Sz 95 (1930–31). fp Frankfurt am Main, 23 January 1933

Transylvanian Dances (Erdélyi táncok), Sz 96, arrangement of Sonatina for piano (1931). fp 24 January 1932

Hungarian Sketches (Magyar képek), Sz 97 (1931, arrangement of Ten Easy Pieces, Nos. 5, 10, Four Dirges, No. 2, Three Burlesques, No. 2, For Children, Book 1, No. 40). fpp Nos. 1–3, 5, Budapest, 24 January 1932; complete, Budapest, 26 November 1934

Hungarian Peasant Songs (Magyar parasztdalok), Sz 100, arrangement of piano pieces (1933). fp Szombathely, 18 March 1934

Music for Strings, Percussion and Celesta, Sz 106 (1936). fp Basle, 21 January 1937

Violin Concerto ('No. 2') Sz 112 (1937–8). fp Amsterdam, 23 March 1939

Divertimento, for strings, Sz 113 (1939). fp Basle, 11 June 1940

Concerto for Two Pianos, Sz 115, arrangement of Sonata for Two Pianos and Percussion (1940). fp London, 14 November 1942

Concerto for Orchestra, Sz 116 (1942?–3, revised 1945). fp Boston, 1 December 1944

Piano Concerto No. 3, Sz 119 (1945). fp Philadelphia, 8 February 1946

Viola Concerto, Sz 120 (1945, completed by Tibor Serly). fp Minneapolis, 2 December 1949

Vocal with Orchestra

Tiefblaue Veilchen, DD 57, for soprano and orchestra, text by C. Schoenaich-Carolath (1899). fp?

Three Village Scenes (Falun, Tri dedinské scény), Sz 79, arrangement of *Falun*, Sz 78, Nos. 3–5, for 4/8 female voices and chamber orchestra (1926). fp New York, 1 February 1927

Cantata profana (A kilenc csodaszarvas: 'The Nine Enchanted Stags'), Sz 94, for tenor, baritone, double chorus and orchestra, text: Romanian *colinda*, arranged and translated by Bartók (1930). fp London, 25 May 1934

Five Hungarian Folk-songs (Magyar népdalok), Sz 101, arrangement of 5 of 20 Hungarian Folk-songs, Sz 92, for solo voice and orchestra, texts: Hungarian traditional (1933). fp Budapest, 23 October 1933

Choral

Est (Evening), DD 74, for male chorus, text: K. Harsányi (1903). fp?

Four Old Hungarian Folk-songs (Négy régi magyar népdal), Sz 50, for male chorus, texts: Hungarian traditional (1910, revised 1912). fp Szeged, 13 May 1911

Two Romanian Folk-songs, Sz 58, for female chorus, texts: Romanian traditional (1915?, completed from draft, B. Suchoff). fp Győr, 16 August 1965

Four Slovak Folk-songs (Négy tót népdal: Styri slovenské piesne), Sz 70, for mixed choir, texts: Slovakian traditional (1916?). fp Budapest, 5 January 1917

Five Slovak Folk-songs (Tót népdalok: Slovácké ludové piesne), Sz 69, for male chorus, texts: Slovakian traditional (1917). fp Vienna, 12 January 1918

Hungarian Folk-songs (Magyar népdalok), Sz 93, for mixed chorus, texts: Hungarian traditional (1932). fp Selection, Kecskemét, 11 May 1936

Székely Songs (Székely dalok), Sz 99, for male chorus, texts: Hungarian traditional (1932, 1938, revised 1982)

Twenty-seven Two and Three-part Choruses, for children's chorus (Vols. 1–6), female chorus (Vols. 7–8), Sz 103, texts: Hungarian traditional, arranged Bartók (1935–6; five transcribed for choir and school orchestra, 1937; two transcribed for choir and chamber orchestra, 1937). fp Selection, Kecskemét, 18 April 1937

From Olden Times (Elmúlt időkből), Sz 104, for male chorus, texts: Hungarian traditional, arranged Bartók (1935). fp Kesckemét, 18 April 1937

Chamber

The Course of the Danube (A Duna folyása), DD 20b, for violin and piano, arrangement of DD 20a (1894). fp?

Sonata, in C minor, for violin and piano, Op. 5, DD 37 (1895). fp?

Pieces for Violin, Op. 7, DD 39 (1895, lost). fp?

Two Fantasias, for violin, Opp. 8-9, DD 40-41 (1896, lost). fp?

String Quartet No. 1 in B major, Op. 10, DD 42 (1896, lost). fp?

String Quartet No. 2 in C minor, Op. 11 DD 43 (1896, lost). fp?

Piano Quintet in C major, Op. 14, DD 46 (1897, lost). fp?

Sonata, in A major, for violin and piano, Op. 17, DD 49 (1897). fp?

Piano Quartet, in C minor, Op. 20, DD 52 (1898). fp?

String Quartet in F major, DD 56 (1898). fp?

Piano Quintet Fragments, DD B10 and B12 (1899). fp?

Scherzo in sonata form for string quartet, DD 58 (1899–1900). fp?

Duo, for two violins, DD 69 (1902). fp?

Albumblatt in A major, for violin and piano, DD 70 (1902). fp?

Andante, in F sharp major, for violin and piano, DD B14 (1903?). fp?

Violin Sonata, in E minor, DD 72 (1903). fpp Movement III only, Budapest, 8 June 1903; complete, probably Budapest, 25 January 1904

Piano Quintet, DD 77 (1903–4). fp Vienna, 21 November 1904

From Gyergyó (Gyergyóból), Sz 35, for reed pipe (*tilinkó*) and piano, arrangement of Three Folk-songs from the County of Csík (1907). fp?

String Quartet No. 1, Op. 7, Sz 40 (1908–9).
fp Budapest, 19 March 1910

String Quartet No. 2, Op. 17, Sz 67 (1915-17).
fp Budapest, 3 March 1918

Sonata No. 1, for violin and piano, Op. 21, Sz 75 (1921).
fp Vienna, 8 February 1922

Sonata No. 2, for violin and piano, Sz 76 (1922).
fp Berlin, 7 February 1923

String Quartet No. 3, Sz 85 (1927). fp Philadelphia,
30 December 1928

Rhapsody No. 1, for violin and piano, Sz 86 (1928).
fp London, 4 March 1929

Rhapsody No. 2, for violin and piano, Sz 89 (1928).
fp Amsterdam, 19 November 1928

String Quartet No. 4, Sz 91 (1928). fp London,
22 February 1929

Forty-Four Duos, Sz 98, for two violins (1931).
fpp Small selection, Mondsee, 7? August 1931;
eight pieces, Budapest, 20 January 1932

String Quartet No. 5, Sz 102 (1934). fp Washington,
8 April 1935

Sonata for Two Pianos and Percussion, Sz 110 (1937).
fp Basle, 16 January 1938

Contrasts, Sz 111, for violin, clarinet and piano (1938).
fpp Movements 1 and 3, New York, 9 January 1939;
complete, New York, 29–30 April 1940 (recording),
Boston, 4 February 1941 (concert)

String Quartet No. 6, Sz 114 (1939). fp New York,
20 January 1941

Sonata, for solo violin, Sz 117 (1944). fp New York,
26 November 1944

Piano

Walczer. Op. 1, DD 1 (1890). fp?

Changing Piece (Változó darab), Op. 2, DD 2
(1890). fp?

Mazurka, Op. 3, DD 3 (1890). fp?

Budapest Athletic Competition (A Budapesti
tornaverseny), Op. 4, DD 4 (1890). fp?

Sonatina No. 1, Op. 5, DD 5 (1890). fp?

Wallachian Piece (Oláh darab), Op. 6, DD 6 (1890). fp?

Fast Polka (Gyorspolka), Op. 7, DD 7 (1891). fp?

'Béla' polka, Op. 8, DD 8 (1891). fp?

'Katinka' polka, Op. 9, DD 9 (1891). fp?

Voices of Spring (Tavaszi hangok), Op. 10, DD 10
(1891). fp?

'Jolán' polka, Op. 11, DD 11 (1891). fp?

'Gabi' polka, Op. 12, DD 12 (1891). fp?

Forget-me-not (Nefelejts), Op. 13, DD 13 (1891)

Ländler No. 1, Op. 14, DD 14 (1891). fp?

'Irma' polka, Op. 15, DD 15 (1891). fp?

Radegund Echo (Radegundi visszhang), Op. 16,
DD 16 (1891). fp?

March (Induló), Op. 17, DD 17 (1891). fp?

Ländler No. 2, Op. 18, DD 18 (1891). fp?

Circus Polka (Cirkusz polka), Op. 19, DD 19 (1891). fp?

The Course of the Danube (A Duna folyása), Op. 20,
DD 20 (1891). fp?

Sonatina No. 2, Op. 21, DD 21 (1891?) Ländler No. 3, Op. 22, DD 22 (1892, lost). fp?

Spring Song (Tavaszi dal), Op. 23, DD 23 (1892). fp?

Szöllős Piece (Szöllősi darab), Op. 24, DD 24 (1892, lost). fp?

'Margit' polka, Op. 25, DD 25 (1893). fp?

'Ilona' mazurka, Op. 26, DD 26 (1893). fp?

'Loli' mazurka, Op. 27, DD 27 (1893). fp?

'Lajos' Waltz ('Lajos' valczer), Op. 28, DD 28 (1893). fp?

'Elza' polka, Op. 29, DD 29 (1894). fp?

Andante con variazioni, Op. 30, DD 30 (1894). fp?

X.Y., Op. 31, DD 31 (1894, lost). fp?

Sonata No. 1 in G minor, Op. 1, DD 32 (1894). fp?

Scherzo, in G minor, DD 33 (1894). fp?

Fantasie in A minor, Op. 2, DD 34 (1895). fp?

Sonata No. 2 in F major, Op. 3, DD 35 (1895). fp?

Capriccio, in B minor, Op. 4, DD 36 (1895). fp?

Sonata No. 3 in C major, Op. 6, DD 38 (1895, lost). fp?

Andante, Scherzo and Finale, Op. 12 (1897, lost). fp?

Three Piano Pieces (Drei Klavierstücke), Op. 13, DD 45 (1897). fp?

Two Pieces, Op. 15, DD 47 (1897, lost). fp?

Great Fantasy, Op. 16, DD 48 (1897, lost). fp?

Scherzo or Fantasie (Scherzo oder Fantasie für das Pianoforte), Op. 18, DD 50 (1897). fp?

Sonata, Op. 19, DD 51 (1898, lost). fp?

Three Piano Pieces (Drei Klavierstücke), Op. 21, DD 53 (1898). fp?

Scherzo in B minor, DD 55 (1898). fp?

Scherzo, in B flat minor, DD 59 (1900?). fp?

Six Dances, DD 60, Nos. 1–2 orchestrated as DD 60b (*c.* 1900). fp?

Scherzo, in B flat minor, DD 63 (1900). fp?

Variations, on a theme by F.F. (Változatok F.F. egy témája fölött), DD 64 (1900-01). fp?

Tempo di minuetto, DD 66 (1901). fp?

Four Piano Pieces (Négy zongoradarab), DD 71 (1903). fpp No. 1, Nagyszentmiklós, 13 April 1903; No. 2, Budapest, 27 March 1903; No. 3, Berlin, probably 14 December 1903; No. 4, Budapest, 25 November 1903

Marcia funèbre, DD 75b, arrangement of two sections from *Kossuth* (1903). fp?

Rhapsody, Op. 1, Sz 26 (1904). fp Újpest, 25 May 1905

Petits morceaux, arrangement of Sz 29/2, DD 67/1 (1905-7?). fp?

Three Hungarian Folk-songs from the Csík district (Három Csík megyei népdal), Sz 35a (1907). fp?

Fourteen Bagatelles, Op. 6, Sz 38 (1908). fpp Baden-bei-Wien, 29 June 1908 (Busoni's piano class); 1–7, 9–14, Paris, 12 March 1910

Ten Easy Pieces, Sz 39 (1908). fpp No. 10, Budapest, 15 November 1909; Nos. 5 and 10, Berlin, 8 January 1910

Two Elegies (Két elégia), Op. 8b, Sz 41 (1908, 1909). fpp No. 1, Budapest, 21 April 1919; No. 2, Budapest, 17 October 1917

For Children (Gyermekeknek), Sz 42 (1908–9 in four volumes, revised 1944–5 in two volumes). fpp 1/19, 23, Szabadka (Subotica), 23 November 1911; selection, Kecskemét, 1 February 1913

Two Romanian Dances (Két román tánc), Op. 8a, Sz 43 (1910). fpp No. 1, Paris, 12 March 1910; No. 2, probably Budapest, 27 March 1911

Seven Sketches (Vázlatok), Op. 9b, Sz 44 (1908–10). fp No. 4, Budapest, 27 February 1921

Four Dirges (Négy siratóének), Op. 9a, Sz 45 (1910). fp Budapest, 18 May 1911

Three Burlesques (Három burleszk), Op. 8c, Sz 47 (1908, 1911, 1910). fp Budapest, 18 May 1911

Allegro barbaro, Sz 49 (1911). fp Kecskemét, 1 February 1913

The First Term at the Piano (Kezdök zongoramuzsikája), Sz 53, eighteen pieces from Piano Method, with Sándor Reschofsky (1913). fp?

Sonatina, Sz 55 (1915). fp Pozsony (Bratislava), 16 April 1920

Romanian Folkdances (Román népi táncok), Sz 56 (1915). fp Kolozsvár (Cluj), 16 January 1920

Romanian Christmas Carols (Román kolinda-dallok), Sz 57 (1915). fp Kolozsvár (Cluj), probably 31 October 1922

Suite, Op. 14, Sz 62 (1916). fp Budapest, 21 April 1919

Three Hungarian Folk-songs, Sz 66 (1914, 1918). fp?

Fifteen Hungarian Peasant Songs (Tizenöt magyar parasztdal), Sz 71 (1914–18). fpp probably Nos. 7–15, Budapest, 17 October 1915; Nos. 6-15, Berlin, 8 March 1920

Studies, Op. 18, Sz 72 (1918). fp Budapest, 21 April 1919

Improvisations on Hungarian Peasant Songs, Op. 20, Sz 74 (1920). fpp No. 7, Budapest, 27 February 1921; complete, Budapest, 18 January 1922

Sonata, Sz 80 (1926). fp Budapest, 3 December 1926 (broadcast)

Out of Doors (Szabadban), Sz 81 (1926). fpp Nos. 1, 4, 5, Budapest, 3 December 1926 (broadcast); Nos. 1, 4, Budapest, 8 December 1926

Nine Little Pieces, Sz 82 (1926). fp Eight pieces, Budapest, 3 December 1926 (broadcast)

Three Rondos on Folk Tunes (Három rondo népi dallamokkal), Sz 84 (1916, 1927). fp Budapest, 29 November 1927

Petite suite, Sz 105, arrangement of Nos. 28, 38, 43, 16, 36 of Forty-Four Duos, Sz 98 (1936, revised 1943). fp Békéscsaba, 6 December 1936

Mikrokosmos, Sz 107, 153 pieces in 6 volumes (1926, 1932–9). fp 27 pieces, London, 9 February 1937

Seven Pieces from *Mikrokosmos*, Sz 108, for two pianos (1939–40). fp Four pieces, Budapest, 29 January 1940

Suite, for two pianos, Op. 4b, Sz 115a, arrangement of Suite No. 2, Op. 4, Sz 34, for orchestra (1941). fp 6 January 1942

Songs

Three Songs (Drei Lieder), DD 54, texts: Heine, Siebel (1898). fp?

Liebeslieder, DD 62, texts: Rückert, Lenau, Goethe (1899). fp?

Four Songs, DD 67, texts: Lajos Pósa (1902). fp?

Four Songs, DD 76 (1903, lost) Székely Folk-song
(Piros alma), Sz 30 (1904–5). fp probably Budapest,
27 September 1957 (broadcast)

Hungarian Folk-songs (Magyar népdalok), Sz 29
(1904–5). fp?

To the little 'Tót' (Slovak) (A kicsi 'tót'-nak), five songs
for voice and piano, Sz 32 (1905). fp?

Hungarian Folk-songs (Magyar népdalok), ten songs
for voice and piano, Sz 33 (1906). fp?

Hungarian Folk-songs (Magyar népdalok), ten songs
for voice and piano, Sz 33a (1906). fp?

Two Hungarian Folk-songs, Sz 33b, for voice and
piano (1906). fp?

Four Slovak Folk-songs, Sz 35b, for voice and piano
(c. 1907, 1916). fp 1-2, probably Berlin, 25 October 1907

Nine Romanian Folk-songs, Sz 59, for voice and
piano (1915). fp?

Five Songs (Öt dal), Op. 15, Sz 61, for voice and piano,
texts: Klára Gombossy, Wanda Gleiman (1915–16). fp?

Five Songs (Öt dal), Op. 16, Sz 63, for voice and piano,
texts: Endre Ady (1916). fp Budapest, 21 April 1919

Slovak Folk-song, Sz 63a (1916?). fp?

Eight Hungarian Folk-songs (Nyolc magyar népdal),
Sz 64, for voice and piano (1907, 1917). fp 6–8, Vienna,
12 January 1918

Village Scenes (Falun), five Slovak songs for female
voice and piano, Sz 78 (1924). fp probably Budapest,
8 December 1926

Twenty Hungarian Folk-songs (Húsz magyar népdal),
Sz 92, for voice and piano (1929). fpp Four songs,
London, 6 January 1930; selection, Budapest,
30 January 1930

Ukrainian Folk-song (A férj keserve: The Husband's
Grief), Sz 118, for voice and piano (1945). fp?

Further Reading

Preference has been given to readers of English, French and German in this short bibliography, but this does not as a result exclude periodicals published in Budapest, such as *Studia musicologica, Documenta Bartókiana* and *New Hungarian Quarterly* which have frequently contained articles on Bartók.

Bartók, B. *Slovenské l'udové piesne / Slowakische Volkslieder*, edited by A. Elscheková, O. Elschek and J. Kresánek (2 Vols., Bratislava, Academia Scientiarium Slovaca, 1959, 1970)

Béla Bartók: Ethnomusikologische Schriften Faksimile-Nachdrucke, edited by D. Dille (4 Vols., Mainz, B. Schotts Söhne, 1965–8)

Rumanian Folk Music , edited by B. Suchoff (5 Vols., The Hague, Martinus Nijhoff, 1967–75)

'Musique paysanne serbe et bulgare du Banat', edited by B. Suchoff (Budapest, 1935) in *Documenta Bartókiana* Vol. 4, 1970

Béla Bartók Letters, edited by J. Demény (London, Faber and Faber, 1971)

Béla Bartók Briefe, edited by J. Demény (2 Vols., Budapest, Corvina, 1973)

Béla Bartók Essays, edited by B. Suchoff (London, Faber and Faber, 1976)

Turkish Folk Music from Asia Minor, edited by B. Suchoff (Princeton, Princeton University Press, 1976)

'Vierzehn Bartók-Schriften aus den Jahren 1920/21', *Documenta Bartókiana,* edited by L. Somfai, Vol. 5, 1977

Yugoslav Folk Music, edited by B. Suchoff (4 Vols., Albany, State University of New York Press, 1978)

The Hungarian Folk Song, edited by B. Suchoff (Albany, State University of New York Press, 1981) [originally *Hungarian Folk Music* (London, Oxford University Press, 1931)]

'Bartóks Briefe an Calvocoressi (1914–1930)', *Studia musicologica,* edited by A. Gombocz and L. Somfai, Vol. 24, 1982

Erdélyi magyar népdalok [Transylvanian Hungarian Folk-songs] edited by B. Bartók and Z. Kodály (Budapest, A Népies Irodalmi Társaság, 1923, reprinted Budapest, Allami Könyvterjesztő Vállalat, 1987)

Magyar népdalok: Egyetemes gyüjtemény I [Hungarian Folk-songs: Universal Collection I] edited by S. Kovács and F. Sebő (Budapest, Akadémiai Kiadó, 1991)

Bartók Letters, The Musical Mind, edited by M. Gillies and A. Gombocz (Oxford, Clarendon Press, forthcoming)

Antokoletz, E. *The Music of Béla Bartók* (Berkeley, University of California Press, 1984)

Béla Bartók: A Guide to Research (New York, Garland, 1988)

Bartók, B. Jnr, 'Béla Bartók's diseases', *Studia musicologica,* Vol. 23, 1981

Bator, V. *The Béla Bartók Archives: History and Catalogue* (New York, Bartók Archives, 1963)

Bónis, F. *Béla Bartók: His Life in Pictures and Documents,* 2nd edn. (Budapest, Corvina, 1981)

(ed.), *Így láttuk Bartókot* [We saw Bartók thus] (Budapest, Zeneműkiadó, 1981)

Citron, P. *Bartók*, 2nd edn., (Paris, Editions du seuil, 1994)

Crow, T. (ed.) *Bartók Studies* (Detroit, Information Coordinators, 1976)

Demény, J. 'Béla Bartók's Artistic Development I', *Zenetudományi tanulmányok*, Vol. 3, 1955

'Béla Bartók's Artistic Development II', *Zenetudományi tanulmányok*, Vol. 7, 1959

'Béla Bartók und die Musikakademie', *Studia musicologica*, Vol. 23, 1981

Dille, D. *Thematisches Verzeichnis der Jugendwerke Béla Bartóks, 1890-1904* (Budapest, Akadémiai Kiadó, 1974)

Fassett, A. *The Naked Face of Genius: Béla Bartók's Last Years* (London, Victor Gollancz, 1958)

Gillies, M. *Bartók in Britain: A Guided Tour* (Oxford, Clarendon Press, 1989)

Bartók Remembered (London, Faber and Faber, 1990)

(ed.) *The Bartók Companion* (London, Faber and Faber, 1993)

Griffiths, P. *Bartók* (London, J. M. Dent, 1984)

Haraszti, E. *Béla Bartók: His Life and Works* (Paris, Lyrebird, 1938)

Juhász, V. (ed.) *Bartók's Years in America* (Washington DC, Occidental Press, 1981)

Kárpáti, J. *Bartók's String Quartets* (Budapest, Corvina, 1975)

Króo, G. *A Guide to Bartók* (Budapest, Corvina, 1974)

'Genesis of Bluebeard's Castle', *Studia musicologica*, Vol. 23, 1981

Lampert, V. 'Zeitgenössische Musik in Bartóks Notensammlung', *Documenta Bartókiana*, Vol. 5, 1977

Lampert, V. and L. Somfai. 'Béla Bartók' in S. Sadie (ed.) *The New Grove Dictionary of Music and Musicians* (London, Macmillan, 1980)

Lendvai, E. *Béla Bartók: An Analysis of His Music* (London, Kahn and Averill, 1971)

The Workshop of Bartók and Kodály (Budapest, Editio Musica, 1983)

Lenoir, Y. *Folklore et transcendance dans l'oeuvre américaine de Béla Bartók* (Louvain-la-Neuve, Institut Supérieur d'Archéologie et d'Histoire de l'Art, Collège Erasme, 1986)

McCabe, J. *Bartók's Orchestral Music* (London, BBC, 1974)

Moreux, S. *Béla Bartók* (London, Harvill, 1953)

Pethö, B. 'The Meaning of Bartók's Secret Path', *Studia musicologica*, Vol. 24, 1982

Ránki, G. (ed.) *Bartók and Kodály Revisited*, (Budapest, Akadémiaia Kiadó, 1987)

Somfai, L. 'Manuscript versus Urtext: The Primary Sources of Bartók's Works', *Studia musicologica*, Vol. 23, 1981

Stevens, H. *The Life and Music of Béla Bartók*, 3rd edn., ed. Malcolm Gillies (Oxford, Clarendon Press, 1993)

Tallián, T. *Béla Bartók: The Man and His Work* (Budapest, Corvina, 1988)

Bartók fogadtatása Amerikában, 1940–45 (Bartók's Reception in America, 1940–45) (Budapest, Zeneműkiadó, 1988)

Ujfalussy, J. *Béla Bartók* (Budapest, Corvina, 1971)

'1907–8 in Bartóks Entwicklung', *Studia musicologica*, Vol. 24, 1982

Books on Hungarian History and Culture

Éri, G. and Z. Jobbágyi. *A Golden Age: Art and Society in Hungary 1896–1914* (London, Corvina/Barbican Art Gallery, 1989)

Hoensch, J. *A History of Modern Hungary, 1867-1986*, trans. K. Traynor (London and New York, Longmans, 1988)

János, A. *The Politics of Backwardness in Hungary* (Princeton, Princeton University Press, 1982)

Mansbach, S. *Standing in the Tempest: Painters of the Hungarian Avant-Garde 1908–1930* (Santa Barbara, Santa Barbara Museum of Art, 1991)

Willet, J. (ed.) and others. *The Hungarian Avant-Garde: The Eight and the Activists*, Hayward Gallery exhibition catalogue (London, Arts Council of Great Britain, 1980)

Selective Discography

Although plans to publish a complete edition of all Bartók's music have yet to come to fruition, a project to record all his work was undertaken by the Hungarian company Hungaroton and was issued on LP, with excellent written commentaries by Bartók scholars such as László Somfai. Parts of this have since been transferred to Compact Disc. Bartók's own recordings, official and otherwise, including fragments of live recordings, were released in this series on two box sets of LPs. The first of these, containing official recordings of (mostly) his own work has been transferred to CDs as *Bartók at the Piano*, Hungaroton HCD 12326–31.

Recordings made by Bartók for HMV, including short piano works, folk-song arrangements and transcriptions for violin and piano with Szigeti have been collected on an EMI CD in the 'Composers in Person' series CDC 5 55031–2. The Washington Library of Congress concert with Szigeti has appeared on CD on a number of labels, including Vanguard Classics, 08 8008 71.

A performance for broadcast by CBS made by the Bartóks of the Sonata for Two Pianos and Percussion, was released on LP, along with some pieces from *For Children* and *Two Easy Pieces*, by Vox Productions in the US, and Turnabout in the UK (TV 4159).

The recording of *Contrasts* made by Bartók, Goodman and Szigeti has appeared on a CBS/Sony CD along with pieces from *Mikrokosmos* on CD 47676.

Performers associated with Bartók include the pianists Andor Földes and György Sándor, and the conductors Fritz Reiner, Antal Doráti, János Ferencsik and Georg Solti; recordings by all of them are included in the list below.

Stage Works

Duke Bluebeard's Castle
Mihály Székely and Olga Szönyi, London Symphony
Orchestra conducted by Antal Doráti; with Berg: Three
Fragments from *Wozzeck*
MERCURY, 434 325–2MM

Duke Bluebeard's Castle
Kolos Kováts, Sylvia Sass, London Philharmonic
Orchestra conducted by Sir Georg Solti
DECCA, 433 082–2 DM

Duke Bluebeard's Castle
Walter Berry, Christa Ludwig, London Symphony
Orchestra conducted by István Kertész
DECCA, 443 571–2 DCS

The Wooden Prince
The Philharmonia Orchestra conducted by Neeme
Järvi; with Hungarian Sketches
CHANDOS, CHAN 8895

The Wooden Prince
Chicago Symphony Orchestra conducted by Pierre
Boulez; with *Cantata profana*
DEUTSCHE GRAMMOPHON, 435 863–2GH

The Miraculous Mandarin
New York Schola Cantorum, New York Philharmonic
Orchestra conducted by Pierre Boulez; with Four Pieces
for Orchestra, Op. 12
SONY, SMK 45837

Orchestral

Kossuth
Hungarian National Philharmonic Orchestra
conducted by Tibor Ferenc; with Concerto for
Orchestra, *Miraculous Mandarin* Suite
PICKWICK, PCD 1013

Rhapsody for Piano and Orchestra
Géza Anda (piano), Berlin RIAS Orchestra conducted
by Ferenc Fricsay; with Piano Concertos 1–3
DEUTSCHE GRAMMOPHON, 427 410–2 GDO2

Rhapsody for Piano and Orchestra
György Sándor (piano), South-West German RSO
conducted by R. Reinhardt; with Piano Concertos 1–3,
Scherzo, Sonata for Two Pianos and Percussion
VOX, CDX2 5506

Rhapsody for Piano and Orchestra
Zoltán Kocsis (piano), Budapest Festival Orchestra
conducted by Ivan Fischer; with Piano Concertos 1–3,
Music for Strings, Percussion and Celesta
PHILIPS, 416 831–2 PH3

Orchestra Suites 1–2
Hungarian National Philharmonic Orchestra
conducted by Tibor Ferenc
PICKWICK, PCD 1028

Violin Concerto No. 1
Kyung Wha Chung (violin), Chicago Symphony
Orchestra conducted by Sir Georg Solti; with Violin
Concerto No. 2
DECCA, 425 015–2 DM

Two Portraits
Montréal Symphony Orchestra conducted by Charles
Dutoit; with *The Miraculous Mandarin*
DECCA, 436 210–2 DH

Two Pictures
Hungarian State Symphony Orchestra conducted
by Adam Fischer; with *Dance Suite*, Hungarian
Sketches, Romanian Dances, Romanian Folkdances
DEUTSCHE GRAMMOPHON, 437 826–2GH

Four Pieces for Orchestra
Chicago Symphony Orchestra conducted by
Pierre Boulez; with Concerto for Orchestra
NIMBUS, NI5309

Dance Suite
London Symphony Orchestra conducted by Sir
Georg Solti; with Concerto for Orchestra
DECCA, 425 039–2 DM

Dance Suite
Philharmonia Hungarica conducted by Antal Doráti;
with Concerto for Orchestra, *Two Portraits*, Pieces
from *Mikrokosmos*
MERCURY, 432 017–2MM

Piano Concerto No. 1
Stephen Kovacevich (piano), London Symphony
Orchestra conducted by Colin Davis; with Piano
Concertos 2–3
PHILIPS, 426 660–2 PSL

Piano Concerto No. 1
Géza Anda (piano), Berlin RIAS Orchestra conducted
by Ferenc Fricsay; with Piano Concertos 2–3, Rhapsody
for Piano and Orchestra
DEUTSCHE GRAMMOPHON, DG 427 410–2 GDO2

Piano Concerto No. 1
Zoltán Kocsis (piano), Budapest Festival Orchestra
conducted by Ivan Fischer; with Rhapsody No. 1,
Piano Concertos 2–3, *Music for Strings, Percussion
and Celesta*
PHILIPS, 416 831–2 PH3

Rhapsody for Violin and Orchestra No. 1
Kyung Wha Chung (violin), City of Birmingham
Symphony Orchestra conducted by Sir Simon Rattle;
with Rhapsody No. 2
EMI, CDC7 54211–2

Piano Concerto No. 2
Maurizio Pollini (piano), Chicago Symphony
Orchestra conducted by Claudio Abbado; with Piano
Concerto No. 1
DEUTSCHE GRAMMOPHON, DG 415 371–2 GH

Music for Strings, Percussion and Celesta
Franz Liszt Chamber Orchestra conducted by János
Rolla; with Divertimento
QUINTANA, QUI90 3052

Music for Strings, Percussion and Celesta
Chicago Symphony Orchestra conducted by Fritz
Reiner; with Concerto for Orchestra
RCA/BMG GD60 175

Violin Concerto No. 2
Yehudi Menuhin (violin), Dallas Symphony
Orchestra conducted by Antal Doráti; with Elgar:
Salut d'amour, Debussy: *La Fille aux cheveux de lin*,
Lalo: *Symphonie espagnole*
RCA/BMG 09026 6 1395-2

Violin Concerto No. 2
Kyung Wha Chung (violin), Chicago Symphony
Orchestra conducted by Sir Georg Solti; with Violin
Concerto No. 1
DECCA, 425 015-2 DM

Divertimento
Ferenc Liszt Chamber Orchestra conducted by János
Rolla; with *Music for Strings, Percussion and Celesta*
QUINTANA, QUI90 3052

Concerto for Two Pianos and Orchestra
Katia and Marielle Labèque (pianos), City of
Birmingham Symphony Orchestra conducted by
Sir Simon Rattle; with Sonata for Two Pianos
and Percussion
EMI, CDC7 47446–2

Concerto for Orchestra
Chicago Symphony Orchestra conducted by Fritz
Reiner; with *Music for Strings, Percussion and Celesta*
RCA/BMG GD60 175

Concerto for Orchestra
Chicago Symphony Orchestra conducted by Pierre
Boulez; with Four Pieces for Orchestra
DEUTSCHE GRAMMOPHON, 437 826–2 GH

Concerto for Orchestra
Cleveland Orchestra conducted by Christoph von
Dohnányi; with Lutosławski: Concerto for Orchestra
DECCA, 425 694–2 DH

Piano Concerto No. 3
see Piano Concerto No. 1

Vocal with Orchestra

Falun
New York Camerata Singers, New York Philharmonic
Orchestra conducted by Pierre Boulez; with *The
Miraculous Mandarin*, Four Pieces for Orchestra
SONY, SMK 45837

Falun
Győr Girls' Choir, Budapest Chamber Ensemble
conducted by Antal Doráti; with Four Old Hungarian
Folk-songs Sz 50, Hungarian Folk-songs Sz 93,
Székely Songs Sz 99, From Olden Times Sz 104, and
Seven Choruses Sz 103
HUNGAROTON, HCD 31047

Cantata profana
József Réti (tenor), András Faragó (baritone), Budapest
Chorus, Budapest Symphony Orchestra conducted
by János Ferencsik; with Concerto for Orchestra
HUNGAROTON, HCD 12759

Cantata profana
John Aler (tenor), John Tomlinson (bass), Chicago
Symphony Chorus, Chicago Symphony Orchestra
conducted by Pierre Boulez; with *The Wooden Prince*
DEUTSCHE GRAMMOPHON, 435 863-2 GH

Chamber

Quintet for Piano and Strings, DD 77
S. de Groote (piano), Chilingirian Quartet;
with String Quartet No. 5
CHANDOS, CHAN8660

String Quartets 1–6
Emerson Quartet
DEUTSCHE GRAMMOPHON, 423 657-2 GH2

String Quartets 1–6
Alban Berg Quartett
EMI, CDS7 47720-8

String Quartets 1–2
Chilingirian Quartet
CHANDOS, CHAN8588

String Quartets 3–4
Chilingirian Quartet
CHANDOS, CHAN8634

String Quartet No. 5
Chilingirian Quartet; with Quintet for Piano
and Strings
CHANDOS, CHAN8660

Sonata No. 1 for Violin and Piano
Gidon Kremer (violin), Martha Argerich (piano); with
Janácek: Sonata for Violin and Piano, Messiaen: Theme
and Variations
DEUTSCHE GRAMMOPHON, 427 351-2 GH

Sonata No. 1 for Violin and Piano
Yuuko Shiokawa (violin), András Schiff (piano);
with Ten Duos (from Forty-four Duos), Sonata for Two
Pianos and Percussion
DECCA, 443 894-2 DH

Sonata No. 1 for Violin and Piano
György Pauk (violin), Jenő Jandó (piano)
with *Contrasts*, Sonata No. 2 for Violin and Piano
NAXOS, 8.550749

Sonata No. 2 for Violin and Piano
Lorand Fenyves (violin), András Schiff (piano); with
Contrasts, Sonata for Solo Violin
DECCA, 443 893-2 DH

Sonata for Two Pianos and Percussion
Katia and Marielle Labèque (pianos), S. Gualda and
J.-P. Drouet (percussion); with Concerto for Two
Pianos and Orchestra
EMI, CDC 7 47446-2

Sonata for Two Pianos and Percussion
András Schiff and Bruno Canino (pianos), Zoltán Rácz
and Zoltán Váczi (percussion); with Violin Sonata
No. 1, Ten Duos (from Forty-four Duos)
DECCA, 443 894-2

Contrasts
see Sonata No. 1
see Sonata No. 2

Sonata for Solo Violin
Victoria Mullova (violin); with Bach: Partita BWV
1002, Paganini: Introduction and Variations on 'Nel cor
più non mi sento'
PHILIPS, 420 948-2 PH

Piano

For Children
Zoltán Kocsis (piano)
HUNGAROTON HCD 12304

For Children
Desző Ránki (piano); with *Mikrokosmos*
TELDEC, 9031-76139-2

Mikrokosmos
György Sándor (piano)
SONY, MPK52528

Piano Collections

Mikrokosmos (selection from Books 5 and 6)
Suite, Op. 14
Romanian Folkdances
Sonata, Out of Doors
Sonatina
Allegro barbaro
Andor Földes (piano)
DEUTSCHE GRAMMOPHON, 423 958-2 GDO

Dance Suite (piano arrangement)
Fifteen Hungarian Peasant Songs
Three Rondos on Slovak Folktunes
Romanian Dances
András Schiff (piano)
DENON, C37 7092

Allegro barbaro
Suite Op. 14 (incl. suppressed Andante)
Ten Easy Pieces
Three Rondos on Slovak Folktunes
Romanian Folkdances
Two Romanian Dances
Peter Frankl (piano)
ASV, CDDCA 687

Fourteen Bagatelles
Two Elegies
Three Hungarian Folktunes
Six Romanian Folktunes
Sonatina
Zoltán Kocsis (piano)
PHILIPS, 434 104-2 PH

Allegro barbaro
Six Dances in Bulgarian Rhythm
Three Hungarian Folk-songs from the Csík District
Fifteen Hungarian Peasant Songs
Mikrokosmos (selection)
Three Rondos on Slovak Folktunes
Sonatina
Balázs Szokolay (piano)
NAXOS, 8.550451

Songs

Five Songs, Op. 15, Sz 61
Five Songs, Op. 16, Sz 63
Five Songs (from Eight Hungarian Folk-songs, Sz 64)
Five Songs, Op. 15 (orchestrated by Kodály)
Five Songs for voice and orchestra, Sz 101 (from Twenty
    Hungarian Folk-songs, Sz 92)
Julia Hamari (soprano)
HUNGAROTON, HCD 31535

Index

Page numbers in italics refer to
picture captions.

Photographic Acknowledgements

The publishers would like to thank the Bartók Archives, Budapest, and Mr Barrie Gavin for their help with illustrations for this book.

Archiv für Kunst und Geschichte, Berlin: 148r, 151
Archiv für Kunst und Geschichte, London: 2, 41, 71, 124, 145, 168, 175, 179, 180, 189, 208–9, 212–13
Bartók Archives, Budapest: 12, 15br+bl, 21, 31, 33, 36–7, 42, 53, 66, 79, 85, 98–99, 106, 140, 144, 146, 147, 148l, 154, 166, 171, 191, 199, back cover
Budapest Historical Museum: 24–5, 48–9
Courtesy of Barrie Gavin: 29, 32, 40, 51, 64, 65, 87, 96, 100, 103, 108–9, 113, 121, 150, 157, 159, 170, 172, 176
Hulton-Deutsch Collection, London: 9, 10, 23, 35, 101, 132–3, 165, 184–5, 187, 188, 204
Hungarian National Gallery, Budapest: 61r
Hungarian National Museum, Museum of Contemporary History, Budapest: 126–7
Interfoto MTI, Budapest: 15tr+tl, 18–19, 56, 57, 114, 115, 130, 169, 194, 197, 215
National Szechenyi Library, Budapest: 11
Range Pictures Ltd, London: 153, 180, 196
Universal Edition, Vienna: 20, 81, 90–1